A
LEGACY of LOVE

A
LEGACY of LOVE

Remembering Muriel Duckworth

HER LATER YEARS
1996 – 2009

edited by Marion Douglas Kerans

For Andrew – who inspires people too! Love, Marion

Roseway Publishing
an imprint of Fernwood Publishing
Halifax & Winnipeg

Editing and text design: Brenda Conroy
Cover photo: Sandor Fizli
Cover design: John van der Woude
Printed and bound in Canada by Hignell Book Printing

Mixed Sources
Product group from well-managed
forests and other controlled sources
www.fsc.org Cert no. SW-COC-003438
© 1996 Forest Stewardship Council

Published in Canada by Roseway Publishing
an imprint of Fernwood Publishing
32 Oceanvista Lane
Black Point, Nova Scotia, B0J 1B0
and 748 Broadway Avenue, Winnipeg, Manitoba, R3G 0X3
www.fernwoodpublishing.ca/roseway

Fernwood Publishing Company Limited gratefully acknowledges the financial
support of the Government of Canada through the Canada Book Fund, the
Canada Council for the Arts, the Nova Scotia Department of Tourism and Culture
and the Province of Manitoba, through the Book Publishing Tax Credit,
for our publishing program.

 Canadian Heritage Patrimoine canadien The Canada Council for the Arts Le Conseil des Arts du Canada NOVA SCOTIA Tourism and Culture  Manitoba

Library and Archives Canada Cataloguing in Publication

Kerans, Marion Douglas
A legacy of love: remembering Muriel Duckworth, her later years, 1996-2009 /
Marion Kerans.

ISBN 978-1-55266-381-3

1. Duckworth, Muriel, 1908–2009. 2. Pacifists—Canada—Biography.
I. Title.

JZ5540.2.D83K47 2010   303.6'6   C2010-902927-5

Contents

Introduction

The news on Saturday, August 22, 2009, that Muriel Duckworth had died in her one hundred and first year set wires buzzing across Canada. People wanted to talk about their experience of her. Some gave interviews to the media; others came together or phoned each other. In the weeks following, memorial services were held at Austin, Quebec, Halifax, Montreal, Ottawa, Toronto and Vancouver. All of us recognized that her passing marked the end of an era, but I sense that we came together not only to remember her but to testify to Muriel's ongoing legacy of love.

In 1996 I was delighted when Fernwood published the biography of Muriel that I had written. *Muriel Duckworth: A Very Active Pacifist* was inspired by my devotion to her. I'd had the opportunity to be close to her for twenty years in Halifax. Muriel caused a significant change in my life, as I am sure she did for many, when in 1978 she introduced me to the peace movement through the Voice of Women, a national peace organization. Muriel became my role model in countless ways. She reinforced the best of my social work education as I watched her practise adult education in both small informal groups and the large organizations she helped to found. Her warm relationships with everyone were at once spontaneous yet carefully tended. Her behaviour was rooted in her principles, and her love for so many individuals reflected her love for humanity. She combined gentleness, tenacity, humour and fearlessness. Muriel became the mother I had never known since my own mother died when I was a young child. I expect she was a mother figure to many other women too. I, among thousands of Canadians, treasured her friendship. We responded by giving the best we had to bring peace to the world.

In the years when I was writing her biography, Muriel was accessible to me at both her home in Halifax and her cottage in Austin, Quebec.

Then I moved away to Vancouver and Ottawa when my husband retired and only saw her for brief periods when we returned in the summertime to our Maritime home. Because I had been spending less time with her, I asked some of Muriel's family members and friends to share their memories of her during the last dozen years of her life. I knew there was more to her story than when I had left off in 1996, and I wanted readers of her biography to know about her closing years. Having reached old age myself, as I read these essays, Muriel remains my model of how an aging lifetime activist can support and inspire younger activists and be a significant elder in her family.

These memories from "near and dear ones" are tales of Muriel's humour, deep affection for her family, outreach to people, ongoing activism despite her advanced age and lasting political "feistiness." They also relate her views on education, religion, death, war and love. As emails and letters poured in and as I re-read the eulogies people had given at Muriel's memorials, I felt called to arrange these memories into a huge bouquet of flowers for presentation to Muriel. This task eased my sad heart whenever I thought I would like to phone her for one of our frequent chats. I hope these beautiful writings bring as much enjoyment and solace to the contributors and the readers as they do to me.

For their pieces, I am grateful to Mariel Angus, Colleen Ashworth, Suellen Bradfield, Fatima Cajee, Jean Cooper, Micheline Delorme, Anna Duckworth, Eleanor Duckworth, John Duckworth, Martin Duckworth, Marya Duckworth, Sylvia Duckworth, Tiffany Duckworth, Sandy Greenberg, Martin Rudy Haase, Marie Hammond-Callaghan, Pat Kipping, Bonnie Klein, Marie Koehler, Megan Leslie, Helen Lofgren, Heather Menzies, Margaret Murphy, Elaine Newman, Marion Pape, Ruth Plumpton, Betty Peterson, Anana Rydwald, Audrey Schirmer, Danielle Schirmer, Norma Scott, Errol Sharpe, Donna Smyth, Barbara Taylor, Gillian Thomas, Maureen Vine, Anne Wonham and Anne Marie Zilliacus. For pictures, I am grateful to Michael Bradfield, Jean Cooper, Micheline Delorme, John Duckworth, Kathleen Flanagan, David Henry, Joan Brown Hicks, Pat Kipping, Terre Nash, Ruth Plumpton, Betty Peterson, Pauline Raven and Maureen Vine.

Errol Sharpe of Fernwood gave me his generous encouragement

when I approached him about doing an addition to Muriel's biography. His patience knew no bounds as I proposed one idea after another. He went one better by offering to publish a separate book. Thus was born *A Legacy of Love*. Beverley Rach, the production coordinator, made my way as easy as possible as she helped me gather pictures and assigned the publishing work. Brenda Conroy, the book's designer, not only caught my editing errors but turned out this beautiful copy. I am also grateful to Nancy Malek for her promotion and to John van der Woude for his design of the book's cover. Finally, I was delighted when Sandor Fizli agreed to let us use his beautiful portrait of Muriel on the cover. He captured her pensive mood, which in turn captures our hearts.

The title of this collection is drawn from my own memory of Muriel when we celebrated her seventy-fifth birthday in Halifax in 1987. Wearing a lovely rose gown, Muriel stood atop a circular coffee table so that she could see everyone in the crowd of over two hundred well-wishers. She thanked us all for coming and said, as she looked around at old friends and new, that she wished she might personally introduce each one of us to the other and tell us how very special every one of us was. She reciprocated our love and wanted to link each and every one of us to the other and to have us all appreciate each other. This is how I personally experience Muriel's legacy of love. When all of us who knew Muriel or wish we had known her join together we will make a difference.

Visiting her one September morning of her last year, I jokingly reminded her that she had said at her seventy-fifth birthday that she wanted to live to be a hundred because she was curious to see how it would all turn out. (I think she hopefully expected that things would get better and that the world would be closer to peace.) Now, she looked at me sadly, shook her head and, on the verge of tears, said, "No, I don't have to live this long to see how it is turning out." Of course she was distressed by the wars still going on, and I was upset with myself for inadvertently causing her to feel this pain. I quickly changed the subject. I wish I had said that she continued to show us the way, although I realize we still have a long way to go to move from war and hatred to love and peace.

Many of us heard Muriel repeat in her later years, "WAR IS STUPID!" and "WHAT THE WORLD NEEDS NOW IS MORE LOVE!" She distilled the wisdom of all her years into the pure gold of these words. And she insisted that we all have to stand up and speak out against injustice and inequality. Muriel, who had given hundreds of speeches, written thousands of letters, organized and attended countless meetings, she who spoke with such moving eloquence, still had a message to convey until her last days. I sense the message is that only love will conquer war. Muriel convinced me that what each of us needs and what the world needs is more love. Joyfully we will spend her legacy as we bring peace and justice to the world.

This collection of remembrances from friends and family about Muriel's later years also contains stories of her earlier life. This series of memories, eulogies and pictures of Muriel is a companion piece to the biography, *Muriel Duckworth: A Very Active Pacifist,* published by Fernwood in 1996. Joining these two books in my mind's eye, I picture Muriel's life as a tapestry where we can trace threads from the beginning to the end, showing us how this ordinary woman became so extraordinary and what made her so beloved and so inspiring to those of us who knew her. For readers not acquainted with the biography, the following is a summary of her life story.

Muriel Helena Ball was born on October 31, 1908, on a farm in the Eastern Townships at Austin, Quebec, the third of five children. When she was nine her family moved to the town of Magog, eleven miles down the lake. Muriel, a shy studious child, grew up loving nature and the rhythm of the seasons. Relatives and friends often gathered in her family's home for hymn sings, card games, good meals and political debates. Her feminist roots went back to a mother who read Nellie McClung, who turned her china cabinet into a bookcase to start up a community lending library and who helped earn the money for her children to go to university by running a tea room and renting rooms to summer boarders.

Muriel credited the Student Christian Movement (SCM) at McGill as the most important part of her university education. She was active in small study groups, in opposing anti-Semitism on campus and in helping raise money for European student relief. At the SCM she met Jack Duckworth. They married the week of her graduation in 1929, and both did graduate studies for the next year at Union Theological Seminary (UTS) in New York. In the vibrant atmosphere at UTS, progressive faculty members were readily accessible to students. It was a time when the "social gospel" permeated theological studies, when the sudden market crash threw the economic system into question, when psychiatric concepts were being introduced and when students were exposed to speakers from other world religions. There was even a beginning dialogue between Christians and Marxists. Students engaged in field work, and Muriel's eyes were opened by her weekly sessions with teenaged immigrant girls at a community church in Hell's Kitchen on the Lower East Side. From this came a lifetime ability to instill confidence in young women.

Returning to Montreal, Jack went to work for the YMCA, and Muriel became secretary to the SCM until their first child, Martin, was born in 1931. She was busy with the family for the next few years, with Eleanor born in 1935 and John in 1938, but found time to involve herself with Jack in the League for Social Reconstruction — forerunner to the Canadian Commonwealth Federation (CCF) and later the New Democratic Party (NDP). Muriel attended the conference that led to the establishment of the CCF. The Duckworth home was the site of meetings for two other organizations, the Fellowship for a Christian Social Order, a graduate version of the SCM, and the Fellowship of Reconciliation, a pacifist organization begun in Britain after World War I. Remembering the lessons of that war, Jack and Muriel actively resisted the advent of World War II. Jack was a declared pacifist, and Muriel supported his stand over the objections of friends and family. Instead of engaging in volunteer activities supporting the war effort, Muriel remained busy throughout wartime starting up children's nursery schools, home and school associations and children's art classes and working with the Canadian Girls in Training. The horror of war touched home when her younger brother Norman, who had joined the Air Force, was killed returning from a raid over France in 1943.

The family moved to Halifax in 1947, when Jack became the general secretary of the new family YMCA. Muriel did volunteer work in community mental health activities and human rights for African Nova Scotians. From 1948 to 1962, she joined the progressive staff of the Adult Education Division of the Nova Scotia Department of Education. She worked full time for the department until she resigned from her paid work in 1967 to become the national president of the Voice of Women (VOW).

Muriel and Peggy Hope-Simpson had started a Halifax branch of VOW in response to a call from Toronto women to form a women's organization to do something about the failure of the Paris Peace talks in 1960. In their first month they called a public meeting to successfully contest the dumping of nuclear waste off the coast of Yarmouth, N.S. The activities of VOW occupied an increasing share of Muriel's attention. As national president, she chaired the Women's International Peace Conference in Montreal in 1967. During her term, the Voices, who opposed the war in Vietnam, captured public attention when they brought three South Vietnamese women from the National Liberation Front to Canada. Muriel accompanied them across the country to packed public meetings in the major cities and at border points between Canada and the United States. There they met with delegations of U.S. women working for peace.Muriel represented VOW at conferences in Paris in 1967, Moscow in 1968, Mexico City in 1975 and Copenhagen in 1980.

Muriel led a delegation of Voices in 1968 to meet the director general of the Suffield Experimental Station to protest Canada's involvement in chemical weapons testing. The women went to explore the agreement between Canada, Great Britain and the U.S. on chemical and biological warfare research and its connection to U.S. chemical warfare in Vietnam.

Muriel was equally at home in small discussion groups and in the full plenary sessions of large meetings. In the early days of VOW Ursula Franklin remarked that Muriel's attendance at meetings meant that standards were ensured. When contention arose she would talk with all parties in a dispute and attempt to come up with a proposal acceptable to everyone. On rare occasions she dissolved into tears.

In 1976 Muriel was a founding member of the Canadian Research Institute for the Advancement of Women (CRIAW), begun primarily by academic women. Muriel became an enthusiastic supporter of the notion of community-based research by and for women. Because she saw CRIAW as a bridge between academic researchers and community activists she remained on the board of directors for five years and was elected president for the years 1979 to 1980.

Muriel gained spiritual strength from becoming associated with the Quakers (Friends) in Halifax in 1962. The simplicity of the Quaker approach, with their silent Meeting for Worship and their view of themselves as searching for the truth, appealed to her. She could relate to a Quaker tenet that there is "that of God in every person" and that each of us has an "inner light" that guides us. Although Muriel and Jack attended the Friends' Meetings regularly and took on responsibility at the Meetings, it was not until 1975, after Jack's death, that she officially joined the Religious Society of Friends. For several years Muriel did not publicly identify herself as a Quaker in her work in the peace movement because she did not want people to think that only Quakers were "for peace" or that you had to be a Quaker "to be for peace." Nevertheless the influence of the Quakers was strong in the Voice of Women as a number of its most active leaders were themselves Friends.

In addition to her volunteer work in the peace movement, Muriel's political involvement in the community expanded when she became one of the founding members of the Movement for Citizens' Voice and Action (MOVE) in Halifax in 1971, and its chair in 1972. This organization began as a citizens' coalition publicly protesting the lack of promised public participation in the Regional Municipal Plan for the cities of Halifax and Dartmouth. During the next six years Muriel was seen as the cement that held together a coalition of broadly based community groups. She was a strong advocate for the interests of the economically marginalized. The education Muriel received in MOVE and the public profile she earned in those years were instrumental in her running for the NDP in the provincial election of 1974, as the first woman candidate in Halifax. While her workload with MOVE was still very heavy, three weeks before the election she agreed to run and, at age sixty-five, undertook the arduous activity of door-to-door campaigning. Muriel received visible support from women and from university students. She did not win but obtained close to 20 percent of the vote in the riding, a previous Conservative stronghold.

Muriel found that she had to work very hard to be taken seriously, even by the men in her own party. On the subjects of education, foreign policy and the status of women she was clearly a leader in shaping NDP policy. She was a prime mover at the federal convention of 1981, where a resolution was passed stating than an NDP government would not participate in the NATO alliance.

The 1980s were filled with Muriel's participation in international meetings for peace. As a pacifist feminist Muriel helped to make Canadian women think about the cost of the arms race and about war as the ultimate instrument of violence against them. Returning from the unofficial parallel conference of the United Nations International Conference on Women in June 1955 in Mexico City, attended by 8000 women, she reported: "On the whole I didn't feel that the people from North America had the same sense of urgency about disarmament as the people did from the developing countries, to whom armament means wars ... They are just destroyed by wars. ... Their progress gets set back by armament.…" At this same conference Muriel led an action of the Canadian women delegates in support of an aboriginal woman, Mary Two-Axe Earley, who was threatened with eviction from the Kahnawake reserve because, according to Canadian law, she had lost her status as an Indian upon her marriage to a white man. The publicity they generated resulted in worldwide support for the cause of First Nations women in Canada.

In 1982 Muriel represented CRIAW at the invitation of the Department of External Affairs on a Canadian women's study tour, with visits to NATO headquarters in Paris and to the Canadian Forces Base in Lahr, Germany. The women were mainly taken to briefings about obscure non-military agencies of NATO. Muriel used many occasions to counteract the propagandist nature of the tour and uncovered the fact that NATO spent less than 1 percent of its budget on non-military activities.

That same year Muriel and Ann Gertler presented a lengthy statement on behalf of VOW to the House of Commons Standing Committee for External Affairs and National Defence. Their evidence showed that militarism deprives women of funds to meet daily human needs.

Over 200 members of VOW attended a giant rally at the United Nations Second Special Session on Disarmament on June 12, 1982, when a million people marched for peace from the U.N. buildings to Central Park. Muriel and Betty Peterson led a delegation presenting a petition of 125,000 signatures of Canadian women across Canada to Gerard Pelletier, Canadian ambassador to the U.N.

After convalescing for almost a year from a near-fatal illness, Muriel went to Japan in August 1983, accompanied by Suellen Bradfield, to attend

Hiroshima Day and the World Conference against Atomic and Hydrogen Bombs. She brought home many moving tales of the Hiroshima survivors she had met. In 1984 she returned to Moscow to take part in the NFB film, *Speaking Our Peace*. Muriel was the soul of the Women's International Peace Conference at Mount St. Vincent University, in Halifax, in June 1985, where 350 women from every continent gathered to examine and advocate women's alternatives for negotiating peace. She had worked tirelessly for nearly two years to support this initiative.

In August 1985 she joined a fact-finding Mission for Peace to Central America at the request of a coaliton sponsored by labour unions, CUSO and Oxfam. As part of the delegation she visited five countries in two weeks, interviewing over a hundred people. She returned home to organize meetings to speak about the information the mission had gathered.

Well into the 1990s, Muriel helped to plan and organize a great many peace demonstrations, marches, silent vigils and petitions. Although she never had to go to jail for her pacifist beliefs, she did land in a federal tax court in 1989, when she was eighty, for withholding about 9 percent of her federal income tax over several years — the portion she figured the country used for war preparations. She argued unsuccessfully: "For two hundred years Canada has allowed young men not to be conscripted if they objected on conscientious grounds.... I feel that neither should my money be conscripted for this purpose."

Anyone who worked alongside of Muriel experienced her energizing force. Muriel was associated with a great many organizations and was one of the founders of seventeen provincial and national groups. Her support to individual women was legendary, her leadership motivating and her encouragement constant. Many institutions recognized Muriel's contributions to adult education, community development, human rights and women's and peace studies. She was given a dozen doctorates from universities across Canada, was a member of the Order of Canada and received the Person's Award and the Pearson Peace Medal. It was typical of Muriel that whenever she was honoured, she managed to turn the award into an occasion for honouring others. When she received the Order of Canada in 1983 she accepted it as a symbol of recognition for the women's peace movement.

Looking back, I see what a great influence an individual may have..... It is individuals who change societies, give birth to ideas, who, standing out against tides of opinions, change them.

Doris Lessing

Never doubt that a small group of thoughtful, committed citizens can change the world; indeed, it's the only thing that ever has.

Margaret Mead

Favourite poster in Muriel's kitchen

Tributes to Muriel

Muriel Duckworth's death on Saturday, August 22nd, brought the following tribute from her friend, noted scholar and peace activist, Ursula Franklin:

> I would like her to be remembered as somebody who demonstrated that it's possible to change one's society, to be profoundly critical and still remain a respected member of that society.

Megan Leslie, Member of Parliament for Halifax, rose in the House of Commons on September 15th, 2009, to pay the following tribute to Muriel:

> As a past recipient of the Muriel Duckworth Award, it is my incredible privilege to rise today to honour the life of Muriel Duckworth.
>
> Muriel Duckworth was known as a wonderful, warm, caring human being. She was also a woman who was tough as nails: a committed activist who called out inequality and intolerance.
>
> In the tradition of the suffragettes, Ms. Duckworth took care of her family while working tirelessly toward peace and justice. She challenged racially discriminating hiring practices. She was a founding member of many grassroots organizations including the Voice of Women for Peace. She joined in the struggle for justice in many areas, including health care, education, day care, and economic development.
>
> But she is perhaps best known for her tireless work integrating pacifism and feminism. She was a pioneer.
>
> And we were so lucky to be able to share Ms. Duckworth's 100th birthday with her this year in Halifax.
>
> Thank you, Muriel. We will do our best to carry on your legacy.

Muriel onstage at the concert for her 100th birthday

A Celebration of Muriel's 100th Birthday

Those of us lucky enough to attend the spectacular concert sponsored by Oxfam Canada at the Rebecca Cohn auditorium in Halifax on that Sunday afternoon, November 2, 2008, in celebration of Muriel's hundredth birthday, will long remember it. The foyer and upper and lower levels were overflowing with a thousand people hailing one another, consuming pieces from a hundred birthday cakes, enjoying retrospective pictures of Muriel's life and especially greeting Muriel. The magnificent performance, *Stand Up ! Speak Out!*, featured spoken scenes from Muriel's life interspersed with choral, solo and group singing. Pat Kipping, the organizer, tells us the story of her relationship with Muriel and recreates for us some of the magic of that memorable afternoon.

Presenting and (Representing) Muriel
Pat Kipping, Halifax

One night after a relaxed supper, Muriel informed me in a matter-of-fact tone: " I plan to live to be 100 and then I'll reassess." I found a secondhand copy of George Burns' silly book, *How to Live to be 100*. We laughed at the irony of a pioneer feminist reading his sexist, boozy, womanizing advice. But I suspect she secretly followed some of the wise tips caught between his wise cracks. And I secretly imagined a 100th birthday celebration. I had just launched my documentary film, *Muriel Duckworth Practising*

Peace (Perversity Productions 1999), which featured her ninetieth birthday celebration. It was hard to imagine how that party could ever be surpassed. The idea of a hundred voices and singing children took hold.

By the time Muriel made her decision to live to 100, our friendship was thoroughly entwined with her actions for peace and justice and my urge to move them beyond small groups and to a wider audience. My first introduction to Muriel was via media. I saw her in *The Wish* (NFB 1970), made by her son Martin Duckworth. I was a teenager in Saint John and aspired to be a humanitarian filmmaker like Martin. That first impression of Muriel as simply "Granny-at-the-cottage" was soon challenged when I recognized her in another film, *Encounter on Urban Environment* (NFB 1971), a documentary about urban renewal in Halifax. "Granny" was also an outspoken woman, standing up in the midst of hundreds of people, speaking out about women's exclusion and boldly questioning military authority. My youthful eyes were snapped wide open.

When I moved to Halifax to work with Reel Life: A Women's Media Collective, my path frequently crossed Muriel's in feminist and activist circles. I still saw her as "old" but beheld her with some awe, even in my youthful radical arrogance. One day, enraged by a CBC radio interview with a war-mongering military "expert" I called on Muriel for advice about how to respond. That's when she wove me into the web of the Voice of Women, skillfully channelling my anger into a broader movement with clear connections between women, peace and social justice. Our friendship took root then and wound through the next thirty plus years like the vines around her apartment walls.

During those years I witnessed Muriel in action at the kitchen sink, on the phone, at meeting tables and dining tables, in the halls of Parliament and on the streets of many cities. She supported the Never Again Affinity Group (NAGS) when our edgy antics made some others in the peace movement uncomfortable. She paid attention to my children and the milestones in my family's life. I fancied we were sisters in a past life. She was a light-hearted and bright presence even during the four years I lived out of the country. Her influence on my perception of people, politics and the planet and how I participate, was gentle but firm and profound.

When Muriel was eighty-five, I witnessed her fierce battle — and it was a battle — against a life-threatening attack of meningitis. Soon after that, I started filming her — just in case she didn't live forever. As the project grew into an hour-long television documentary, I felt privileged yet burdened with a huge responsibility. I would represent this well-known and well-loved woman to people who knew her better and for

Pat Kipping and Muriel, June 2009

much longer. I would introduce her to total strangers, not always sympathetic. Most daunting, I would represent Muriel to herself. Thankfully, I was guided by Muriel's now-famous quote, "If it's worth doing, it's worth doing badly." *Muriel Duckworth Practising Peace* has been in circulation for a decade. Like most human endeavours, it has flaws, but Muriel accepted it as another way to spread her prevailing message of peace, love and action. Through the film, people of all ages and political stripes have met the "venerable peace veteran" for the first time, or have become reacquainted. I hope it keeps encouraging people to find their own way to a sustainable activist life, with Muriel's as an inspiration.

When Muriel reached her late nineties, she was lucid and healthy with unwavering commitment to her ideals. Surprisingly, I found myself working for Oxfam Canada, an organization that Muriel had supported since its founding in the 1960s. She served on the Oxfam board in the 1970s, led a peace delegation to war-torn Nicaragua in the 1980s and was a monthly donor for decades. Muriel was Canada's most enduring "Oxfammer." Oxfam's intensified focus on women's rights and active citizenship aligned beautifully with Muriel's persistent life themes. Her 100th birthday was a rare chance to celebrate the enduring quality of those themes for achieving social justice and community development with one who lived the example.

Muriel and her family embraced the idea. Oxfam established the Jack and Muriel Duckworth Fund for Active Global Citizenship, a lasting tribute to Muriel and her husband, an activist pacifist in his own right and major influencer and supporter of Muriel's activist life. The official launch of the Duckworth Fund would be on Muriel's hundredth birthday, and it was my paid job to make it happen! I had a budget, skilled help and fantastic volunteers.

Cakes arrive from the Valley. L to r: Chris Toplack, Andrea Lynne, Elaine Eye, Heather MacDonald

Muriel was active in the year-long concert planning process, selecting songs and suggesting performers. She loved the idea of a concert that connected her life and Jack's to Oxfam's work. Even as her energy and independence dwindled that year, Muriel was engaged with the planning and delighted to hear news of the growing Duckworth Fund. Jack had been very successful at raising funds in his time. She talked frequently about Jack, who had been gone for thirty-five years. She was happy that more friends were learning about him.

Muriel and the planning committee insisted that the concert celebrate the people, the movements and the communities that inspired Muriel and that were, in turn, inspired by her. The arts and artists would be central. Strengthening hope and inspiring people to take action for the future would be essential. Each song, performer and reader, each selection of Muriel's words were chosen with great care

Peggy Hope-Simpson prepares to serve some of the 100 birthday cakes

Muriel and her granddaughter, Marya Duckworth, greet an old friend at the reception for her hundredth birthday concert. As usual Muriel pays close attention.

and held deep meaning for Muriel, her family and those close to her. I urge readers to find the words to the songs and ponder the meanings they held for Muriel or let them inspire.

Before the concert, Muriel was able to greet most of the thousand people who crowded into the Sculpture Court at the Dalhousie Arts Centre at a coffee and cake reception. Friends from as far away as England and El Salvador, mixed with others from all over North America. There were a hundred cakes, each baked or provided by a different person. Politicians, performers, children, grandparents, friends and family all contributed. It was a giant cake potluck!

Stand Up! Speak Out!

Stand Up! Speak Out! The Muriel Duckworth 100th Birthday Concert begins with Mi'kmaw activist Cathy Martin gathering the audience with her drum and leading Muriel into the auditorium. On stage, Cathy and the We'koqma'qewiskwa singers from Cape Breton perform the traditional gathering song, welcoming us to the space and this sacred land.

As the audience stands for the Honour Song, the stage is bare except for We'koqma'qewiskwa and the rows of chairs at the back that will gradually fill with a hundred diverse and powerful voices. A beautiful portrait of Muriel is projected on the wall behind the performers. Near the podium we see Muriel's shawl, draped on a coat rack. One of the drummers, a Mi'kmaw elder, presents the shawl to a girl child, who reads the first of Muriel's words: "*We had three tall pine trees in front of the house, and I remember thinking that the tops of the trees touched the sky. What I thought the sky was, I don't know, but the trees touched the sky. And then at the foot of the hill was a lake. So there you were between the lake and the sky. It was really lovely.*"

Now Muriel's daughter, Eleanor, performs a solo dance to kd lang's song "Simple," sung by fourteen-year-old Erin Brocklehurst. "And love as

Anna Duckworth reads her grandmother's words

"Simple" singer, Erin Brocklehurst, Eleanor Duckworth, dancer

philosophy is simple…and ours." The audience is simply awed.

Host Olga Milosevich introduces the theme of concert, quoting Muriel, "*To bring about the changes we need in society, all of must speak out and act.*" Olga explains that all the readings are Muriel's words, spoken, written or reported at various points in her life. Throughout the concert, each reader at the podium will wrap herself in the shawl, symbolically becoming Muriel to reveal some pivotal moment in her life or one of her key messages. Photos will be projected throughout the concert.

What follows is the edited script from that day with a disclaimer about acknowledgement. Muriel was rigorous about including and recognizing each individual's contribution. I learned the importance of that from her. The concert involved 150 volunteers, including performers too numerous to name here. They were roundly thanked in the printed program at the concert and afterwards. In the interests of simplicity and space I have left out many names. I apologize and hope no one is offended.

Muriel's words: *For a farmer's wife, my mother did remarkable things. She emptied our china cabinet and put books in it and made a little lending library. She read Nellie McClung, fed hungry people off the train, welcomed homeless young girls, raised money to start a seniors' home* *and was very active in the church. She believed she could have some effect, and she did.*

The year 1925 was very important in my life. That autumn I entered McGill University and became involved in the Student Christian Movement, which was quite new. For the first time in my life I had a teacher who sat in a circle with us and asked questions that challenged our preconceptions. She would not tell us the "right answer." This was the beginning of my adult search for truth and my sense that all things must be open to me. It was unsettling. It was painful. It was exciting.

Music: "Poisoning the Student Mind" — Truro Youth Singers

Muriel's words: *At McGill I fell in love and married Jack Duckworth, a theology student. We were married in 1929 and went as students to Union Theological Seminary in New York City. At Union the social gospel had a strong appeal. So did pacifism. That's where we learned about the Fellowship for Reconciliation, the first interfaith peace organization in the United States. We returned to Montreal in June 1930 feeling that by working with children and young people we would be on the growing edge of the church and we would help build the Good Society.*

I used to hear that people felt sorry for Jack that he had a wife like me. But he didn't take it seriously and the children didn't take it seriously. The only thing that bothered him was if his shirts weren't ironed or his socks weren't mended. And that sometimes happened because I couldn't always do the washing on Monday, the ironing on Tuesday, the mending on Wednesday and the cleaning on Thursday. They had to be fitted in. The things I really wanted to do outside the home had to be done when the children were at school. Other things got done around that. But Jack was very supportive. He would say, "You can do it if anyone can." He could have squashed me. He was a very, very strong character. People called him the most aggressive pacifist they had ever seen. He was very strong.

Tony Fry gave a moving tribute to Jack Duckworth, who had mentored Tony during his youth and inspired him throughout his life.

Music: "To Be a Pilgrim" — David Roback with the Truro Youth Singers

Muriel's words: [accompanied by "Hummingbird Chorus" from *Madama Butterfly*, sung by the Aeolian Singers] *Saturday afternoon at the*

Opera was broadcasting on the CBC when Martin was a baby. Being in with the baby, I started listening. I knew nothing about it but I began to love the music. I like Il Traviata. I love Carmen. Butterfly still makes me cry. These quizzes they have between

Alexa McDonough reads Muriel's words

the acts are wonderful because you can pick up so much. I really have given myself a sixty-five-year course in opera by listening every Saturday afternoon, and it's free!

My consciousness of women as women had an awakening through the founding of the Voice of Women in 1960. Letters poured in from thousands of women who joined the Voice of Women. We were afraid and angry. Afraid of the imminence of nuclear war and angry that politicians and military men could do this to us, create this threat. Would we just sit and cry? No, we would not! We organized. We found our voice.

Music: "Last Night I Had the Strangest Dream" — Clearing by Noon

Muriel's words: *It was* Encounter on Urban Environment *in the early sixties and they brought twelve men to Halifax talking about what it was like and what was wrong with it and what it should be like. I got up and made a nice, polite little speech about the fact there weren't any women up there and they laughed. This was a joke. I said, "You're not taking me seriously." Then they tried to get a little serious about it but they didn't know how.*

Music: "Bread and Roses" — Clearing by Noon

Muriel's words: *We must not think of human rights as vast problems "over there" about which we can do little. We must remember that we have problems in our province, on our doorstep, and there IS something we can do.*

Music: "Feed the People" — Cheryl Gaudet with Scott MacMillan and Clearing by Noon

Music: "Sisters, You Keep me Fighting" — Aeolian Singers

Muriel's words: *Three times in the last three years, I have spent about two weeks with the Vietnamese women. The last occasion was in July when I travelled across Canada with Madame Dung from the Mekong River area, Madame Cao from Saigon and Madame The from Hanoi. They met hundreds of Americans in Canada who came across the border to talk with them or who were already here as draft resisters or deserters. If Canada seeks to play a more active part in finding solutions to conflicts, our governments must take action to end the tragedy of Vietnam.*

Music: "My Heart is Breaking" — Aeolian Singers with Marsha Coffey, percussion

Muriel's words: *In 1974, I was the first woman in Nova Scotia to run for political office at the provincial or federal levels. The CBC announced that a "65-year-old housewife" was the NDP candidate for Halifax Cornwallis. That upset my friend Johanna Oosterveld. She wrote in a letter to the newspaper: "A 65 year old housewife indeed! Muriel Duckworth is an experienced educator and an internationally known and respected representative of women's rights. She is knowledgeable and concerned about many issues and has and is spending a great deal of time working with community groups in Halifax. She is a housewife and mother just as much as men are gardeners or repairmen or fathers — no more, no less. I am disturbed enough that no more women are running in this campaign. It's disgraceful to have the CBC dismiss them as housewives."*

Music: "Listen to the Voices" — Carolyn McDade and Gaia Singers

Muriel's words: *War is the greatest destroyer of human life, the greatest polluter, the greatest creator of refugees, the greatest cause of starvation and illness. We all have to care, not just for our own little circle, but for the whole universe*

This is part of a poem by Adrienne Rich that I keep on my refrigerator: "My heart is moved by all I cannot save. So much has been destroyed. I have to cast my lot with those who, age after age, perversely, with no extraordinary power, reconstitute the world." There will always be work to do to change the world.

Music: "My Heart Is Moved" — Carolyn McDade and Gaia Singers

Muriel's words: *I grieve for the lies that were told and repeated and made their way into editorials. And most of all I grieve for the completely*

unjustifiable, and there-fore wholly tragic deaths of these men, women and children, health workers, teachers, farmers, friends and families of people I met in Nicaragua — death from the hills that look so friendly until you know that at any moment a band

Lynn Jones reads Muriel's words

of murderers, trained and armed by the United States, may come down on your village or your school or hospital or health centre. These are the tired, the poor, the huddled masses yearning to be free.

Music: "Set Her Free" — Aeolian Singers

Robert Fox and Elizabeth Church, representing Oxfam Canada, explained the idea behind the Jack and Muriel Duckworth Fund for Active Global Citizenship and the work it would accomplish as people continued to contribute.

Muriel's words: *The movement is strong because the peace movement and the women's movement, the environmental movement and the human rights movement now understand that we need each other. It has taken a few years for this sense to emerge, that we can and must rely on each other. I particularly like Oxfam's approach of promoting democratic development. The approach is one based on principles of equality, justice and respect — principles that are essential if there is ever to be peace in the world.*

I've always found it hard to define God…I can relate to George Fox's idea that there is "that of God in every person." If you believe that there is that inner light of God in you, then you must grant that there is that inner light in other people.

Music: "A Light Inside" — Truro Youth Singers

Muriel's words: *I am attempting to be guided by my conscience after the manner of the Quakers since the seventeenth century. Since I was twenty years old I have been strongly opposed to war and the threat of war as a means of dealing with international affairs.*

I joined the Quakers when I was sixty-six — after a lifetime as a

Truro Youth Singers enjoy the full sarcasm of "Poisoning the Student Mind"

member of another church. I hold in deep respect the Quakers' reliance on inner conscience rather than on outside authority as the guide to one's life decisions. Finally, I realized that to be consistent with my religious belief, I could not allow my money to be conscripted for war. I must withhold it, because I would not myself take up arms. How could I sit comfortably at home writing cheques to make it possible for others to do the killing? [Long pause to let that question sink in. Reader takes off the shawl.] "And now, to honour Muriel's Quaker practice that she carried into dozens of public silent vigils, we will have a moment of silence."

The audience observed a moment of silence in recognition of Muriel's Quaker tradition and the many silent vigils for peace she initiated.

Muriel's words: *The Black community in Nova Scotia is the one I feel very close to and involved with. And I'm angry. Things are better than when we moved to Nova Scotia in 1947, but there still are nasty feelings of discrimination. But Black people are not standing for this anymore. They are doing something about it. The rest of us have to support them in whatever way we can.* [Pause] *I'll never forget the day that Nelson Mandela was released from prison. It was so exciting! Everyone walking to Cornwallis Street Baptist Church. It was a wonderful atmosphere!*

Music: "In My Soul" (Inkuleko Iyeza), "Dream Deferred" and "Freedom Has Beckoned" — Four the Moment.

Muriel's words: *I love to sing, I'm awful at it but I sing along with the opera when no other people are around. Sometimes I just can't help it.*

Just a few of the Nova Scotia Raging Grannies singing "Muriel's Song"

I sing with the Raging Grannies too. When the G-7 was coming here everybody said, "You've got to have some Raging Grannies!" Just a few phone calls and we did it.

Music: "Hello Muriel" — Raging Grannies

Muriel's words: *I remember the first time I heard about people buying futures. I couldn't believe it. That people would buy futures on wheat, on food, the essential thing that everyone has to have. What right does anyone have to buy futures on food?*

Music "I Know Something about the Economy" — Raging Grannies

That was the biggest gathering of Raging Grannies I had ever seen and they completed the hundred voices on the stage. It was time for the grand finale with Muriel on the stage. While she was wheeled out of her comfortable seat in the theatre and around to the stage, Delvina Bernard and Four the Moment got the audience dancing and exercising their voices with rousing rounds of "Happy Birthday to You" — the Stevie Wonder version, written for Martin Luther King Jr. The auditorium rang with improvisation and joy. When Muriel arrived on stage, surrounded by nineteen family members, she was overjoyed and almost speechless.

We presented Muriel with her surprise gift, a performance of "Muriel's

Delvina Bernard and Four the Moment teach the world to sing
Happy Birthday, the Stevie Wonder version

Muriel joins in singing her song

Grand Finale — "Muriel's Song"

Song," commissioned for her hundredth birthday. The composers and assembled hundred voices, including the fresh voices of the Truro Youth Singers, performed it beautifully, accompanied by piano and guitars. And then everyone sang it. The earth was alive with her song.

Muriel's Song

Voices calling, rising, falling,
And the earth is alive with your song.
Children dreaming, starlight streaming
And the earth is alive with your song.

We will stop these stupid wars,
The hatred and the lies.
We will light this darkest hour and not be terrorized.

Fire burning, planets turning
And the earth is alive with your song.
Loving, growing, giving, knowing
That the earth is alive with your song.

In your name we'll carry on
Speaking out for everyone
And honour all that you have done
With passion and with grace.

Voices calling, rising, falling,
People dreaming, starlight streaming,
And the earth is alive with your song.

© Rose Vaughan and Cheryl Gaudet 2008

(For more information about the concert and the Duckworth Fund visit
www.oxfam.ca and enter "Duckworth" or "Stand Up! Speak Out!" in the
search box. On the concert page, there are links to videos of some of the
performances, including "Muriel's Song".)

Who and What Kept Muriel Going

Throughout her life Muriel was a powerful advocate for all those who live with inequality: people who are poor, people with a mental illness, children, parents, women, gays, First Nations, people of African descent and the many victims of war and violence. Muriel was always on the side of those who lacked power as she insisted that there had to be solutions to society's problems. With her radical thought and gentle language she persuaded many who came into contact with her by her well-reasoned positions on how to create a "fairer "world.

A number of persons who wrote to me referred to Muriel's own favorite quotation from Adrienne Rich, "My heart is moved by all I cannot save…" Several years ago Muriel sent out this stanza in her own handwriting inserted in her Christmas letter. Many of us mounted it on our refrigerator doors just as Muriel had done. Like a chorus this verse comes back to me as a love song we might all sing about Muriel.

Muriel's capacity for creating community was legendary. Her gift for relating personally to each individual initially drew people to her and in turn drew them together for action whenever she called upon them. And call upon them she did! Muriel used the telephone as readily as this generation uses the Internet. This habit never diminished with the passing years. It both kept her in touch with people and drew people around her, responding not just to her personal charisma, her undivided attention and ability to empathize, but to her call to "do something" to make this a better world.

Muriel never really retired from her career as "a very active pacifist."

She went on participating in her favourite activities. Until her last year she attended public meetings, sponsored an annual women's retreat at her cottage, sang with her beloved Raging Grannies and went to meetings of the Voice of Women and to many social occasions. People told me how, long past the age of ninety, Muriel's life continued to be a rich one. This was reflected in both her papers and correspondence, whose organization she oversaw at the end of her long live. Yet always at the centre of her activities were the deep friendships she cultivated and went on cultivating.

Our Busy Lives
Betty Peterson, Halifax

In later years, living in the same apartment building for almost twenty years, we relaxed over things we enjoyed — world figure skating, the Oscars and hot political debates on TV — our telephone wires were hot! We were political junkies, interested in everything at all levels. And as Muriel had no other regular means of transportation since the early 1980s, we often sat in my car, coming home late at night, and we'd look at each other… "Are we crazy or what?" and we'd laugh.

Thankfully, we continued going to all events through 2005–06: Raging Grannies, NDP events, VOW meetings and days of renewal, with

Betty Peterson with Muriel, 2008

grand reunions from all over N.S., labour budget watches and many more. As well through Rudy and Mickey Hasse, we went to symphonies, Neptune Theatre, NDP and environmental fundraisers. Muriel wanted to go to everything, me too. And we did — walker and all.

One of the most memorable things about Muriel's last five to ten years were the gatherings in her apartment on Sunday nights. Often there was a specific reason: a planning session, a documentary film or news clip, a serious sharing of what we each had been doing or sometimes just for fun and warm womanly support and encouragement. Muriel got on the phone, and who knew who would be coming. Those arriving early took over the kitchen for refreshments, and latecomers cleaned up. And Muriel was the centre of it all. We left encouraged and uplifted.

Women's Annual Retreat

Anne-Marie Zilliacus, Ottawa

I used to go to Muriel's cottage whenever I was going to Halifax. Muriel always said the cottage was on the way to everywhere, which was true if you took the long way round. It was like an oasis. A lovely old spot on the Lake Memphramagog, like a little piece of the past. Her cottage was nearly as old as Muriel, built when she was just a little girl. It is a real old-fashioned cottage with a large porch looking over the lake and rocking chairs for everyone to sit and watch the hummingbirds. I travelled there with my children, with friends, by myself. Everyone was always welcome, and there were always interesting people there who had dropped by for tea or were staying for a couple of nights — also on their way to somewhere else.

Even in her nineties, a time when many others have taken a step back to take a well deserved rest, Muriel was not content to step back. She wanted to share her wisdom and experience. In July 2001, she was invited to a gathering of wise women at the Women's University in Norway. The gathering brought women from various countries, ages and backgrounds together to ask them to think and dream deeply of our past and futures and to ask themselves what is necessary to our survival on this precious earth. They wanted to look at women's solutions to overcome the problems of war, climate change, economics, violence.

There were twenty-four women at the conference (Muriel, then ninety-two, was the oldest), strong feminists all, and they were in Norway to contribute to and promote a renewal of feminism in the construction of knowledge and inspire each other to take this model of feminism home to their own communities. Muriel was bursting with enthusiasm about the conference when Jane Orion Smith and I were at the cottage that summer. Muriel wanted to share her experience, to try and give an opportunity for the women she knew to have a space of tranquility where they could talk in the same way about peace, globalization, all the things that affected their and our lives, and then go back to their lives refreshed, inspired, ready to continue their struggles. Orion and I were eager to help her and thought we could have a similar conference at Muriel's cottage. It was the summer of 2001, and then came September 11th. It was obvious what the first topic would be — Empire. We saw empire as a living reality unfolding in our communities and nations. September 11th had brought us abruptly into a world where we faced a permanent "war on terrorism," which we felt would bring terror into all our lives.

The next July we sent out an invitation to about twenty women to come to Muriel's cottage. We planned an informal program, scheduling the time but not the content. We told the participants we wanted to build the program together, and they should come with thoughts of discussions they would like to lead or take part in, presentations they could give on their own work or thoughts and resources they could share. We sent them some queries for reflection before the weekend to help them prepare their hearts and minds for our time together.

Muriel wanted the group to be as diverse as possible, to include young and old, professional and student, women who could come and be inspired and refreshed and then go back to their lives invigorated for the struggle to make the world a better place. She wanted to share the passion and enthusiasm that had informed her own life, using her greatest gift, friendship. When women come together in groups like we did in those gatherings there is intimacy, laughter, tears, stimulation. The discussions are free ranging, the atmosphere gentle and nurturing. That first summer we were a group of mothers, daughters, sisters, friends, and even though we did not all know each other at the beginning we were definitely friends. We were women who were university professors, artists, musicians, students, teachers, activists, filmmakers, nurses.

Our gathering that summer was quite wonderful. I particularly re-

Muriel at the annual Day of Renewal of the Voice of Women, Nova Scotia, c. 2005

member the closing activity, when Eleanor called us together standing in a circle and asked us to share the story of what inspires and drives each one of us. As the circle of stories ended, Eleanor repeated a phrase and gesture from each one, asked us to repeat them together and turned it into a dance. Fantastic.

That weekend became the first in an annual event, and for the next six years Muriel would telephone Orion and me every spring to plan the topic and think about whom we would invite for the next gathering. It was different every year, a different topic, some different people, but always there were fascinating conversations and that precious opportunity to spend time with Muriel — always so generous with her friendship.

The Halifax Raging Grannies

Maureen Vine, Dartmouth

As soon as Muriel heard about the establishment of the Raging Grannies in Victoria in 1987, she began to talk about them. She knew many of the B.C. Grans because they were peace activists involved with the Voice of

Women. She observed that their street-theatre approach to getting out the peace message gained the attention of both the public and the media in a way that briefs, petitions and letters to the editor never could. Muriel is quoted in the press as saying: "I'm a Raging Granny because I felt it was a good way to make people think in other ways about what's going on in the world" (June 2000, *Halifax Chronicle Herald*).

The Halifax Grans' very first gathering was not a meeting but an action, an "Anti GST Party," with songs, hats, costumes and a symbolic dumping of the GST into Halifax Harbour — as per the historic Boston Tea Party. It was a great success, with the *Daily News* giving front-page coverage. Even with that success it would be another few years before Muriel finally found a few women willing to meet for the specific purpose of organizing the Halifax Raging Grannies. That meeting at the Halifax Library included Eva Munroe and Marion Pape, who together with Muriel and Betty Peterson became the dynamic foursome that led and nurtured the Halifax Raging Grannies.

Muriel's and Betty's lifetime of peace work was a major resource to the Grans, and though many of us had known them for years, we were unaware of their considerable knowledge of music. They made sure we had the information we needed to write good songs, and they also made sure our singing was good, or at least in tune and the words clear.

Not surprisingly many of our early outings were peace actions. In the cold of February 1995, we gathered outside a Halifax Liquor Store, led by Muriel, and sang out in protest of continued nuclear testing by France. It was part of a world-wide protest-boycott of French wine. It worked. The testing stopped within six months.

Soon the Grans were in full action mode with many, many events to attend in support of peace, social justice and the environment. Muriel was there, very much one of the "old bats, in funny hats, and activists at large." It was work, but it was fun too.

Early in 1998, Muriel broke her hip. The peace community rallied around, ensuring that her meals and other needs were taken care of. Ever the thoughtful activist, even while convalescing, she sent a lovely note of thanks and encouragement to the Grans, quoting a song, "Don't let our hearts be broken. Don't let them weaken our will. Don't let our hopes be

Raging Grannies, foreground l. to r: Elinor Reynolds, Betty Peterson, Evelyn Monroe, Muriel and Helen Lofgren, background: Dorothy Jackson and Barb Dacey 2001–02

vanquished; *And don't let our voices be still.*" The last line she underlined and she signed, "Love, hope and courage to you all." She recovered and we had the great joy of singing at her ninetieth birthday party later that year.

Muriel and the Halifax Raging Grannies flourished. In 1999 the Grans received the Greater Halifax/ Dartmouth YMCA Peace Medal Award. We knew we were on the right track when we received a thank-you note in March 1999 from Canadian Federation of Students, students of the Nova Scotia College of Art and Design and the International Socialists: "Thank you for giving your voices, all your voices, and your time, your experience and above all else, your hope. Solidarity between young and old, student and worker, woman and man, parent and child, town and country, will save us all."

In 2002, with the leadership of Muriel, Betty Peterson and Elinor Reynolds, we organized and hosted the Raging Granny Unconvention for ninety Raging Grannies from across the country. It was a huge task. When we faltered a little, Muriel was there with a note of advice and encouragement: "The World needs the Raging Grannies — and how! We can't help the world by ourselves, but we can do a lot by being well informed, loving and caring and ready to support others in the ongoing struggle to change the world." The Uncovention was a wonderful success. It wasn't long after that talented and creative Grannies groups were established in Wolfville, Nova Scotia, and in Charlottetown, P.E.I.

Through her nineties, though she was tiring, Muriel continued her many peace activities, including the Grans. She attended as many gigs as she was able. When George Bush came to Halifax, she led the march with the help of a wheelchair and friends. She never missed an opportunity to get people thinking about the decisions our governments are making on our behalf. Sometime in her last year she told a reporter that as long as she was here she would do what she could to take us toward a better world. Commitment! When she couldn't attend we always felt her spirit of peace with us, as it is today.

October 31, 2008, was Muriel's hundredth birthday. At her party, thirty Grans from Halifax and Wolfville were on hand to sing "Hello Muriel." We sang with love and pride, especially Gran Hazel Lawrence, who was wearing Muriel's old evening dress. We loved her, she loved us; it was our very best gig ever.

"A Song for Muriel," by the Halifax Raging Grannies (written in the 1990s), tune: "Hello Dolly"

Telephone rings....rinnnggg!
Hello, it's Muriel
Can't say no to Muriel
When she calls you up to get some peace work done.

Wendy Lil, Maureen Vine, Muriel, Fatima Cajee, Anne Mueke (behind Muriel), 2004

We'll take a stand, Muriel
Hand in hand with Muriel
We'll be reaching, we'll be teaching, we'll be standing firm.
So now the world's changing
For the good, changing
Muriel's showed us how to shake the status quo.
So, grab your hats, Grannies
No time to stop and chat, Grannies
Time to take on the government
Time to shake up the establishment
No such thing as retirement
For Muriel.

Involving Women in Peace

Sandy Greenberg, Halifax

It was as a peace activist that I knew Muriel best. Her home was always open for women to gather for meetings, to view videos, to discuss issues, to write letters. Her walls were full of paintings and her apartment full of plants, as well as books, a piano, teapots and china, and inspiration everywhere — doves, sculpted words of "Peace" and "Hope" and posters and wall hangings with words such as, "What if they funded education, and the military had to hold bake sales," and "War is not healthy for children or other living things."

During the Ethiopian famine, I went to an event and saw Muriel Duckworth and Betty Peterson there. I decided that if they were in the Voice of Women, it would be an organization I would feel comfortable joining. I had been in radical political organizations during the late sixties and found that they inevitably ended up being led by men who took power and directed everyone else. I was right that the Voice of Women was a non-hierarchical group of women, where there was always an atmosphere of inclusion and respect.

Muriel never had a computer, but she did master the art of writing down email addresses, without the spaces between the words, as she was

Muriel at VOW protest against the Afghan War, c. 2005

always up for a challenge. Her mode of communication was her voice — either over the phone or in person. If a letter needed to be written, a politician needed to be persuaded, a meeting needed to chaired or notes taken, an event planned, a petition circulated, she would gently ask someone directly, "Would you be able to do that?" or "Would you be willing to do that?" Of course, the answer she usually got was "Yes."

Muriel would go to every peace lecture or event, even though her aging body was weary, her joints ached, and it was complicated for her to get there. Her good friend, Pat Kipping, who would often drive her, said Muriel explained why she kept going: "If people see me there, it will encourage them to keep going to these gatherings."

There were many facets to Muriel's life, and at her memorial service, people spoke of her spiritual life as a seeker and a Quaker and her roles in the lives of others as a family member, educator, friend and mentor, lover of art and nature, anti-poverty activist, anti-racism activist, feminist, community development organizer, political organizer and pacifist and peace activist.

Many people have commented on how Muriel could make you feel that you were truly seen and appreciated. Shortly after her death, I visited one of the Internet sites where people could comment on an article about Muriel's life and her passing. A man had written, "She lived to be a hundred, so she didn't have any friends left." How wrong he was. Muriel has the most friends of anyone I have ever known. Muriel has hundreds, probably thousands of friends, and each one feels like her best friend. We also feel like her daughters and granddaughters. We miss her.

Rich Friendships
Fatima Cajee, Halifax

As I sit here remembering my times with Muriel, a smile naturally appears on my face. I am so happy to have had the opportunity to know Muriel in my lifetime. She has enriched me and made me a better Muslim and by default a better human being. We were friends, Muriel and I, we spent time together doing different things. One thing we did was to have lunch together once a month. We'd go out to different places and walk arm in arm and talk, eat, laugh. Sometimes I'd take lunch over to her apartment. When I arrived the table was laid beautifully with two place settings, one for me and one for her. These were such special times, Muriel and I together sitting and talking. At one such lunch Muriel asked if I wanted to have tea, I said yes, but I would make the tea. She took me into her little kitchen and showed me how to make a good cup of tea; she told the history of her beautiful teapot, which was very old. After tea we'd sit on the sofa and talk, these were the most precious times for me because Muriel and I cried together and laughed together as we shared stories of our lives and the state of the world. She related the history of events and was always

Muriel and Fatima Cajee

concerned about violence and our inability to solve problems with non violent means. We talked long about such matters.

Other times Muriel would call and ask if I was free to take her to the dentist or to the bank; at other times it was the ophthalmologist or the hairdresser or a drive to a meeting or to attend a talk at the university; and so I took her and cherished the time spent. She had these Sunday evening get-togethers at her apartment where we watched documentaries or movies on peace and non-violence.

Yes! Non-violence and peace — it was this that most affected me in our relationship and had the most impact on me. In her I had an example of what it means to be Muslim (which is to attain peace with oneself, with God, with the God's creation — humans, plants, animals, the ecology). To attain peace with all and everything; is it not what Muriel was about?

On one occasion I took lunch over to Muriel's, and we had Betty Peterson come and join us. I took sandwiches and baked fresh scones. It was delightful to be there with them, me a Muslim woman from South Africa, Betty a draft dodger from the USA, and Muriel the peace activist from Magog. Then it was prayer time for me, so I asked leave to say my prayers. Muriel and Betty sat quietly with me until I finished my prayers; they shared my prayers with me.

Ohhhh, how lucky I feel to have had these times alone with Muriel — the lessons of love, of peace, of non-violence, of laughter and tears. These are what all humans are about, is it not? There were times when I felt really sad and hopeless about the state of the world. At such times Muriel always said that there is always something we can do. For me, that something to do at such times was just to be with Muriel and know that being together, we two very different women comforting and consoling each other was peace in the making.

In the summer when Muriel retreated to Magog, we had lunch before her departure. During the summer we'd call each other and Muriel would sometimes mail a note to me. In 2003, I received an envelope in the mail addressed from Muriel. Inside was a card with a picture of little girls from different races in playful togetherness, and the front of the card read:

The only way we are ever going to ensure peace on this planet is to adopt the entire world as "our family." We are going to have to hug them, and kiss them. And dance and play with them. And we are going to have to sit and talk and walk and cry with them. Because when we do, we'll be able to see that, indeed, everyone is beautiful and we would all be poorer without each other. — Stan Dale

On the inside here is part of what Muriel wrote:

Dear Fatima, When I saw this card in a store in Magog (looking for a card for a great-granddaughter), I just *had* to buy it for you. I miss you and think of you often. Today another terrible speech, full of lies from Bush. If I didn't know a lot of wonderful people, some very special ones like you, working for peace and justice, I would be very depressed. I have a real hope that the world can be saved but it won't be easy, will it? Much love Muriel

An Environmentalist Too

Martin Rudy Haase

When Mickie and I and our three sons decided to emigrate to Canada because of the Vietnam War, a colleague at the Cambridge office of the American Friends Service Committee told me that the "peace person" in Nova Scotia was Muriel Duckworth. A few days after moving to Chester in 1967 we went to Halifax to meet Muriel, who was then living in "the Hive," the Duckworth's home, always buzzing with activity. She was very cordial, and from that day on we became ever closer friends.

Muriel's concerns were wide-ranging, and when she learned I was planning to establish Friends of Nature in Canada, a conservation society I had founded in 1954 to save a wild island on the Maine coast from being "pulped," she joined immediately. Many environmental organizations don't oppose war, but she was pleased that Friends of Nature considers war and preparation for war the greatest threat to the environment.

In 1988 I had the pleasure of accompanying Muriel on a sea trip to New Zealand, where she was cordially received in the Quaker communities of that nuclear-free country. During the sixteen-day voyage we discussed

Taken in June 2009 at the swearing-in ceremony of the first provincial NDP government in N.S., Maureen Vine and Alexa McDonough (background), Muriel and Norma Scott

many things, and I gained an even greater appreciation for her wonderful dedication to so many good causes.

During the campaign in Nova Scotia in the early 1980s to stop planned uranium mining and to establish a moratorium, Muriel was a very active participant, and she kept up the pressure on successive Liberal and Conservative governments for a legally binding moratorium. At the Mount St. Vincent memorial in celebration of her life on September 27, 2009, the new NDP premier told me his government would finally pass a law banning uranium mining to honour Muriel. They did so, thus making Nova Scotia the first jurisdiction in the world to make uranium mining illegal.

Organizing Muriel's Papers

Marie Koehler, Halifax

I first met Muriel around 1980, during the protest against uranium mining in Nova Scotia, when I was living in Forties Settlement, only 17 kilometres from the site of the exploratory mine. Gillian Thomas and Donna Smyth were among the organizers of that protest, and they kindly drew my family into their circle.

Lunch in Muriel's cozy nook with Dorothy Allan, Joan Hicks' ninety-four year old mother

One night we were invited, on one of the darkest days of December, to be part of a St. Lucia day celebration. The guests waited in our hostess's dark basement until, with fanfare, it was lit by a pale-gowned Muriel descending the stairs with a wreath of flaming candles on her head. All my subsequent memories of Muriel are infused by that image — the Christmases, Boxing Days or Thanksgivings at Donna and Gillian's, Voice of Women protests in front of the Halifax Library or at the Grand Parade, and birthday parties with Betty Peterson or other large events. Muriel was one of my heroes.

So when Donna and Gillian mentioned to me that Muriel needed someone to help sort her papers, it was easy to say yes. I had barely begun when it was time for Muriel to spend the summer at her lake, but in the fall of 2007 we started in earnest, with me arriving every Thursday at 9:00 a.m. and staying, usually, until noon.

I was at sea, a sea of paper. My ability to sort my own paper is abysmal — I had no idea how to sort Muriel's. Gillian came to the rescue (again), suggesting that I buy banker's boxes and label them according to Muriel's passions. Most of these passions overlapped with one another, but eventually there were more than a dozen categories, including Voice

of Women, feminism, Quakers, peace (general), environment, international development, friends, family, writings (about Muriel), writings (by
Muriel), NDP, honours, etc.

All of these papers were stored in the small guest room in Muriel's
apartment, stuffed in large shopping bags behind the chair, on the chair,
under the desk, under the bed, crammed onto shelves, stacked in the
closet, and some, very clearly organized, in a full four-drawer filing cabinet, which I left as they were. I loved the way Muriel had saved envelopes,
stamps and writing paper — so frugal. Some of the bags were organized
by year, some by subject — all full of the most wonderful fragments of a
very large life. What a privilege!

When I began, Muriel, always gracious, would offer me breakfast, ask
me about myself and talk, sometimes for an hour. I gradually realized
that this was tiring for her, and the work was not progressing, so most
days I would arrive, exchange hugs, make sure she didn't need anything
and disappear into the spare room. Eventually, our greetings became very
short, which she told me was a relief, since she still had a lot to do, and it
was tiring to talk. Sometimes I would arrive to find the night guest, one of
dozens organized to stay over to ensure that if Muriel got up during the
night she didn't fall, still talking with Muriel, but hours of talking often
required a nap when the guest had gone. And yes, everyone wanted to be
loved, and was loved, by Muriel.

My categorizing, which was a kind of pre-archiving, never failed to
fill me with awe and gratitude for such a well-lived life. In these bags was
voluminous correspondence to Muriel from wonderful people around
the world engaged in peace, development, environmental advocacy and
spiritual awakening, and from Muriel to family and friends. I found one
letter to one of her aunts, written when she was sixteen and in her first
few weeks at university, apologizing for the letter being short because she
had been so busy; it was eight pages long.

Initially, I would bring some cards and letters to Muriel to look over
before I boxed them but stopped when I realized she was throwing them
away. I rescued these, thinking that all these pieces of her life had value
and that some day someone would put them together. There were the
obvious biographical elements — courses she had taken, notes on policy

issues, speeches she had given, honorary degrees, thank-you notes, requests for appearances and other high-profile activities. And there were intensive communications with family and friends and acknowledgments of private donations and hundreds of kindnesses by Muriel.

Muriel at 100 with Marie Mutananga at the cottage

We had fits and starts of organizing — she to go to the lake, I to look after my own affairs, but gradually the papers filled up the boxes and there were only books and magazines to distribute. When Muriel moved to assisted living, Eleanor invited the archivist to remove the boxes. He didn't know Muriel and had no idea of her importance in the world of feminism and peace. I urged him to keep the boxes labelled Friends as well as the more conventional categories, because Muriel's life had been lived large for a hundred years, and a hundred years from now the connections inherent in her friendships around the world would be a valuable resource to someone looking at our times.

Muriel, Betty Peterson and Ed McCurdy, composer of
"Last Night I Had the Strangest Dream," 1997

Muriel with Robert Fox, executive director of Oxfam Canada, at Muriel's home
with one of the main messages of her later years

Aging and Home Care

As Muriel's body aged, she was subject to several falls, careful though she was to avoid these. She faithfully practised the exercises physiotherapists gave her. Late in life she was delighted to learn the proper way to get out of bed. Muriel seldom complained but she would admit with a certain impatience how quickly she tired and how much sleep she seemed to need. Yet she insisted on getting exercise. When I visited her at her cottage I would accompany her as she laughingly struggled with her walker to climb the unpaved hilly road up to her mailbox, stating that it was good for her.

Gradually family and friends surrounded her with circles of love and care from the community she had previously drawn around her. Women, in particular Suellen Bradfield, Helen Lofgren and Norma Scott, were always there for her and helped to organize daily care and, in her ninety-eighth year, all-night care as well. They enlisted a small army of willing volunteers who responded to the invitation to stay an overnight with Muriel. Invariably this also meant having fun and enjoying good conversation with her.

On Becoming a "Handmaiden"

Norma Scott, Halifax

Before Christmas 2007, Muriel, Eleanor and I had a conversation about Muriel's need to have someone to assist her with daily chores and schedules. I was invited to be her personal assistant. I was touched. You see, I consider her the Queen of Peace and here I was being asked did I want to be her handmaiden? Well of course I did! I had the privilege of being in this role for nearly six months. I stayed with her for several hours during three to four days a week, and daily checks by phone became the norm as well.

During this period our friendship was enriched at many levels, deep personal levels. And we had so many laughs. At one phone check-in, Muriel professed how tired she was. She had kept herself awake for a good part of the night trying to remember if she was ninety-nine or a hundred. I assured her she was indeed ninety-nine, and we had a good laugh.

Early in the New Year, it became obvious after another fall that Muriel would need someone to stay overnight. After exploring the cost of home care, she and I came up with the idea of volunteer friends who would be asked to become Muriel's "crew" — her overnight visitors. And so began the "keep Muriel in her apartment as long as possible cause." We developed a list of friends who were available for overnights when the family was not available or in town. Everyone was very generous with their time; some even felt honoured to be asked. Muriel was awed at such an outpouring of support and help. Also many of Muriel's friends were very generous with supplies of cooked meals and cookies etc., which always amazed and delighted her.

Given her age we did at times talk about death and dying. The last time we discussed it, Muriel was pondering what to do after her hundredth birthday. She suggested that some older people simply stop eating, and I said, "but Muriel you like your food too much for that!" She replied, "Well I guess I'll just keep on going." We both agreed that would be for the best, and the subject seem to resolve itself — after we had a good laugh.

Muriel continued to want time to herself, but there were times when I knew no one had been with her for a couple or more hours, when the walk down the corridor of her apartment building seemed so long. I kept

Norma Scott, Muriel and Zimel Zhang, 2007

hoping she was alright. Relief would wash over me as I walked in to find Muriel sitting in her chair watching TV.

A Night with Muriel

Errol Sharpe, Boutilier's Point

In March 2008, Norma, my old friend and bridge buddy, asked me if I would stay with Muriel one night. I considered it a great honour to be asked and readily agreed.

When I knocked on Muriel's door around seven in the evening, she was expecting me and called out, "Come in, the door is open." Muriel was sitting in a big armchair, obviously ready to have a chat. She was pleased to see me and we began by catching up with the news of our families. Muriel spoke of her daughter Eleanor and how she was still teaching at Harvard University, her sons Martin, in Montreal, and John, in Kingsburg, Nova Scotia. She spoke of her grandchildren with great pride and specifically talked about John's daughter Alex, who was an accomplished snowboarder. I got Muriel caught up on my partner Beverley, through whom I had come to know Muriel some twenty years before, our son Jesse, who was finishing foundation year at Kings University College in Halifax, and Myah, who was in junior high school and living at home in Boutilier's Point. Muriel also enquired about my two older sons, who were living in Toronto, and asked about our publishing company. I had brought along a book I thought she might enjoy. The interests that Muriel expressed to me were about the present. At ninety-eight years old she had not regressed into the world of her past. She did comment, one might even say complain, that her memory was not as good as it once was and that she could not read as much as she once could. I thought to myself, "if you're complaining about your memory at your age, at age sixty-eight, I should be absolutely devastated about my own fading capabilities."

When I asked Muriel what time she went to bed, she told me about nine o'clock. Then the conversation focused on current events and world affairs. Muriel was concerned about the wars in Iraq and Afghanistan. We shared our disgust and consternation at what was going on in the world. As was often the case with Muriel, the topic of discussion turned to peace. Muriel wanted to know what I thought of war. I told her honestly that while I abhorred war, armed resistance might well be necessary to stop the scourge of capitalist expansion and save the planet. We then talked about the massive world protests against the United States' invasion of Iraq. I said to Muriel, "It is hard to imagine a more massive international protest than that waged against the invasion, and the United States invaded anyway." She said she thought that these governments were not going to change no matter how many people opposed them. She advanced the idea of massive organizing at the local level. I was amazed. Here was a woman who had "fought" for peace and "fought" to change the course of government for as many years as I had lived, calling for a new strategy. We spent some time talking about the need to build from the bottom up, to take over control of our own communities, our own resources and our own lives. As we spoke, discussed and even disagreed, I was astonished by the clarity of Muriel's thought and the grasp she had of contemporary issues and conditions.

Muriel's stated bedtime passed and I wondered if I should remind her of it. However, she showed no indication of tiring. She had found

Errol Sharpe and Betty Peterson

someone with whom to talk politics and world affairs, and she was not going to waste the opportunity.

Finally at ten-thirty I did mention the time. Muriel seemed surprised that it was so late. She remarked as to how she did not get many chances to talk politics and thanked me for our discussion, saying, almost as if it was her duty, that she should now go to bed. When I told her that I would most probably waken around seven, she made sure I knew where to get food for breakfast and told me that she usually got up around nine. Expressing concern that she might awaken me if she had to get up during the night, she went to bed.

I remember going to bed and sleeping soundly. If Muriel did get up I did not hear her. It occurred to me in the morning that my being in Muriel's spare bedroom was of no material use to Muriel. She could have tumbled on the floor, and I most likely would not have heard her. However, I did feel that my presence and our long discussion were immensely important to Muriel.

I got up around seven, prepared myself some cereal, made a coffee and read a book while waiting for Muriel to get up. Shortly after nine she came into the room. After she got a bit to eat, the conversation of the night before resumed, this time over a cup of coffee — I think Muriel actually had tea.

When I had agreed to stay the night at Muriel's I was not sure what

Muriel with two of Errol's children, Myah and Jesse Rach-Sharpe

to expect. Although I had known Muriel for twenty some years I had never before spent time with her alone. My time with her was always in the context of a social event, a march for peace, a telephone call urging me — an urging that was more like a command — to come out to a rally, or arranging a visit with Beverley and the children. On that night in April 2008 I gained a new appreciation of Muriel. I had read, and published, her biography written by Marion Kerans, and knew of her keen mind, powers of observation and global knowledge. But talking to Muriel that night was like talking to a person many years younger, a person very aware of the world she lived in and still very determined to do what she could to change it.

Muriel told me that evening that I was the only man that had stayed over with her. I later heard that she gleefully told friends how she had spent the night with a man. For this man it was a great privilege, a great inspiration and a great thrill. Muriel Duckworth is a person I will always remember with great fondness and great admiration. She was a living example of what we all should aspire to be. To have had the honour of knowing her and being in her presence will forever be an important part of my life.

Friendly Care

Helen Lofgren, Halifax

Over the years and because it was relatively convenient to do so, I came to drive Muriel to women's events, peace events, Voice of Women meetings, NDP events and eventually Raging Grannies. We shared the same wonderful family doctor, so it seemed natural to take her to those appointments, too. Then there was the rotation that developed some years ago to take her to her weekly physio sessions in the swimming pool at the Rehab Centre. In the summer when she'd broken both her hip and her pelvis in two different falls at her cottage in Austin, I became part of a rotation of drivers.

Our friendship deepened that summer when she'd had those falls as I'd visited her in the hospital. In fact the first fall had happened the day I arrived in Austin by bus, so I had to return to Montreal and ended up visiting her in hospital there. I remember going out to buy fruit and yogurt for her. She knew it was important to eat well and "keep regular" as she said. It was around then that she was getting to know my daughter, Emily, and she became very interested in Emily's development as a young composer, the kind of interest she's always shown in young people. Over the years they developed their own close friendship, and there was never a time Muriel didn't say, "Tell me, what is Emily doing these days?"

Later that summer, returning to Austin, we learned that Muriel once again had fallen and was in the local Magog hospital. There we found her cheerful, alert and quite chagrinned to have fallen again. As we were on our way back to Nova Scotia, we were also giving a ride to another musician friend, who lived in NB. He came to visit Muriel with us too, and together the three of us surrounded Muriel and sang to her a healing chant. She was very moved by the chanting, which really is very lovely and healing. We camped out overnight at the cottage and visited her again the next morning before being on our way. I remember Muriel telling me then how discouraged she felt at being immobilized again, how easy it would be to "slip away," I think she put it, and how she had to struggle with herself to keep busy with reading and writing letters. Writing wasn't easy though, as she had cut her right hand along the outside edge and it

Colleen Ashworth, Suellen Bradfield, Muriel, Norma Scott, Linda Christenson-Ruffman, and Helen Lofgren on Muriel's 99th birthday

pressed uncomfortably on the stitches as she wrote. Her determination prevailed and she wrote anyway!

Just when the family wanted to be sure she never was alone through the night at Magog, Muriel met the wonderful Micheline Delorme. Micheline wanted to work on her English. For years, Micheline came at 9 p.m., they had tea together, went to bed after listening to the 10 o'clock news, and had breakfast together before Micheline left at 9 a.m. She soon was another member of the family. Once Muriel left the hospital, Michelene offered to come to stay with her nights unless Muriel had family or visitors staying overnight, to help her up the stairs and back down again in the morning, and in case help was needed at night. That relationship continued over the years, Michelene coming at nine, tea together and conversation, with Michelene practising her English and Muriel always pleased to be working on her French, her major so long ago at McGill.

It was through those visits with Muriel at the cottage, and other times as well that were just peaceful and uneventful, overflowing into our time in Halifax, that our relationship came to have an increasingly personal dimension, not unlike some aspects of extended family. Muriel invited both Emily and me to participate several times in her Wise Women Weekends at her cottage. These were wonderful cooperative events to get together, meet new wonderful activist women, share and relax.

Later I became one of the regulars who stayed with her overnight. Whenever I went there for the night, I brought supper, which we shared again, generally inviting Betty. Muriel was delighted with these suppers and in spite of increasing difficulty in getting around, already had set the table with her lovely old china with the delicate pink flowers, lovely old silver that was always polished, and the old pink etched wineglasses. Elegant, indeed!

In the morning after spending the night, I always prepared a special breakfast. Often it was her favourite kind of porridge, steel-cut oats soaked overnight, then cooked in the morning, with maple syrup on top, and fresh fruit salad. After breakfast and cleaning up, or doing any little thing Muriel might need, I returned home generally tired, having slept with "one eye open" in case she might need me. She never did. Though I kept the door open and often heard her get up, I had the feeling she was being extra quiet to not disturb me! Who was looking after whom?

Le don d'allumer les êtres

Micheline Delorme, Magog

J'étais souvent auprès de Muriel à son chalet pendant les quelque dix dernières années de sa vie. J'ai été frappé par sa façon d'agir avec les personnes, son respect. J'ai vu défiler des gens de toutes sortes à sa table ou devant son feu de foyer, des gens engagés politiquement ou socialement, impliqués auprès des sans-voix, des intellectuels et des créateurs, des jeunes qui en étaient au choix de leur orientation de vie, des petits-enfants qui ne savaient pas encore combien était spéciale leur Granny, si pleine de compréhension pour les mentalités qui changent vite, et ces gens que le service amenaient chez elle, tous accueillis comme si leur passage était l'événement le plus important de sa journée. Sa présence, sa qualité de présence à l'interlocuteur, alliée à son magnétisme personnel en faisaient une hôtesse charmante, qui avait le don d'allumer les êtres. Personnellement, en sa présence, je me sentais exister bellement.

Connaissez-vous une femme de 95 ans qui s'occupe de faire réparer le toit, couper un arbre, changer le chauffe-eau, envoyer des fleurs, réserver des billets de train, qui monte un escalier de 17 marches — bien comptées — pour rejoindre sa chambre à coucher, qui lit The Gazette du samedi, de bout en bout? Bien sûr, elle a fait cela toute sa vie, mais à cet âge, on se repose, non? Muriel ne le voulait pas.

D'autres auront souligné la force et la cohérence de ses convictions en faveur de la paix, de la promotion des femmes, du soutien aux sans voix. Par exemple, cette grande fête à Halifax pour ses 100 ans, était-elle une fête pour elle ou plutôt pour les bénéficiaires d'Oxfam? Elle y a salué personnellement des centaines de personnes. Un tel geste de générosité me coupe le souffle. Mais il s'inscrit dans toute une vie d'implication sociale.

Quel trésor luit en moi, hérité d'elle? Elle m'a donné beaucoup de bonheur par le simple rayonnement de la bonté de son cœur. Et voilà que j'ai envie d'en faire autant pour ceux que Dieu met sur ma route.

Thoughts on the Closing Time
Suellen Bradfield, Halifax

September 2007: We visited Muriel at her beloved cottage in Magog where she had spent the summer. Its restorative magic could be seen in Muriel's "yes, we are blessed beyond measure" spirit. Her mobility was challenged, but with her walker she moved independently around the cottage.

Our conversation that day revolved around political events, grand-children (hers and ours) and wonderful past experiences. As always, I was moved by Muriel's knowledge of current events and her desire to take action to effect change. There was never a suggestion that she had done her share and now it was our turn.

Our visit was short. Muriel's energy at ninety-eight was impressive but knowing she needed a quiet time to rest, we left shortly after lunch. As we prepared to leave, Muriel moved to her rocking chair on the veranda, with book in hand, for quiet reflection.

October 31, 2007: Muriel turns ninety-nine. Michael and I hosted a small birthday party at our home. The morning of the celebration, I realized that the three steps into our home would be impossible for Muriel. One year had made a big change in her mobility. The walker was now a necessity and stairs were a big challenge. Michael built a railing and Muriel got up those three steps with determination.

The guests were mainly friends who took Muriel to her many health appointments, did grocery shopping and cooked special meals. We had great fun that day, and her warm laughter was infectious. The conversation was lively and Muriel made sure it was not all centred on her.

Muriel and Suellen Bradfield at the cottage

We presented Muriel with a bright pink T-shirt with the number ninety-nine on the back and a peace symbol on the front. We declared her the Gretsky of the social justice movement.

Spring 2008: The months following her ninety-ninth birthday became increasingly challenging for Muriel. In the spring, she wanted a change. Her family found an excellent assisted-care facility, and Muriel was delighted to move into an apartment at the Berkeley. She could see the Bedford Basin from her living room but preferred to call it the Atlantic Ocean. Her spacious bedroom accommodated her beautiful plants and wonderful family photographs. It was a happy transition.

Summer 2008: In 2008 Muriel again summered in Magog, returning to Halifax in the fall to celebrate her hundredth birthday.

She was experiencing more health challenges and extreme tiredness. She spoke of her loss of energy in terms of "not being much good for anything." This was hard to hear, but I would counter that she had to listen to her body and leave the demands of the world to those whom she had inspired. This included the many media people who interviewed her for her hundredth birthday and would frequently remain to absorb more of her inspiration and insight after they turned off their tape recorders. Even at a hundred, she was not taking a sabbatical!

Muriel did not fear death but she did not welcome it. Life was too precious. She loved people and wanted to stay connected to family and friends. Her capacity to love was simply amazing. It was only in the last weeks of her life that she was willing to let us go, telling us to love each other.

Muriel's Gift of Being Present in the Moment
Heather Menzies, Ottawa

During the last weeks of Muriel's life, I joined a tag team of friends and family who took turns being with Muriel in the small, old, francophone hospital in Magog, where she was sent to recover after breaking her leg. She'd fallen within days of getting to the family cottage on Lake Memphremagog, a pilgrimage she made most summers of her adult life to swim, visit with friends and family on the verandah, and renew her energy for the activism to which she devoted so much of her life. I realize now how sharing the small ordinary actions of each day with Muriel, and observing her in them, taught me some of the fundamentals of that devotion.

Taking my cue from her daughter Eleanor, with whom I stayed at the cottage, I arrived each morning with a handful of day lilies picked from the sward of wild meadow that runs from the cottage down to the lake, and every morning, Muriel feasted on them with her eyes, saying how lovely they were and how kind I was to have brought them. Then, taking further cues from Eleanor, whose devotion to her mother expressed itself in myriad ways including a commitment to supplement the meagre hospital meals, I washed a handful of blueberries, and sprinkled these liberally on the hospital-issue cornflakes. Muriel smiled indulgently at this fussing and diligently lifted one slow, shaky spoonful after another to her mouth. We listened to classical music on the radio and talked about

Heather Menzies sharing her book *Enter Mourning* with Muriel

mutual friends. She chatted with the scrawny, toothless older man in the bed opposite and with the nurses who came to change her and hoist her into a sling and, from there, into a wheeled geriatric chair so that we could go for a walk. She seemed to have all the time in the world, because she took the time. Once I was reading out loud from one of the books she was currently reading: Barack Obama's autobiography, *Dreams of my Father*. I was at the part in which he wrote about his mother and the struggles she'd had. She stopped me and asked me to read a certain passage again. I did. "Ah," she said and, having gotten it, nodded for me to go on. There she was, open to new ideas even then and there. Present in the moment, making it full, realizing its fullness with her presence.

That was her genius and, to me, how she embodied the peace she sought in her activism. She did this in being so present in the moment with everyone she encountered that whoever she was talking with not only felt as important as anyone else, but also believed that what they shared in that moment really mattered. Her commitment to equality, to social justice and compassionate conflict resolution was, I think, a corollary of this — this fundamental openness and willingness to engage, with a simple question launching a conversation.

One day when two nursing aides arrived after breakfast to change Muriel's linens, I noticed that one of them, a very young woman, was new. I stood back and watched them work, rolling Muriel this way and that, often jarring her injured leg, and as usual I marvelled at how bravely Muriel endured this. When the ordeal was over, Muriel reached out and took the young woman's hand in hers. She looked up into her face, smiled that lovely loving smile of hers, and asked: "And what is your name?" The young Quebecoise nursing aide answered shyly, a radiant smile lighting up her face as she looked at Muriel and perhaps squeezed her hands in response.

Muriel taught me to open the portals of myself to others, to lead with love and to trust no matter what. When I can say "I love you" with the spontaneity, generosity and frequency with which she did, I will have arrived. I hope her example can live on in me, encouraging me to be fully human — and then to act so that our world and planet can be a place in which all humanity and all creation can flourish in peace and harmony.

Muriel's Influence on Friends of Every Age

Muriel's influence was at the heart of the messages people sent me. Young and old, women and men recalled her inspirational presence among them and what she meant to the peace movement, the women's movement and the citizens' movement at the international, national and local levels as well as to them personally. Scarcely anyone who came to know Muriel remained quite the same as before. She taught many of us to be activists, and we became more sensitive to human need and to social justice.

Muriel, My Namesake

Mariel Angus, Ottawa

(*Editor's note: Mariel is my granddaughter and is named for both Muriel and me*).

Muriel was already in her late seventies when I was born, so the opportunities I had to get to know her were for the most part during the last ten years of her life.

When I was in high school, I visited her a few times in the summer at her cottage near Magog. It was at a time when I was first becoming interested in activism and social justice, and I wanted to get to know my half-namesake more personally.

She would always welcome us warmly and would often pull out recent articles from her bookshelf about one social issue or another and share her thoughts with me on them. We would usually spend our visits by the fireplace in her living room, chatting about life in general and social activism in particular. I always enjoyed looking at the walls of her cottage; the peace march posters and activism slogans that covered them, some of which were from decades ago, gave me a visual sense of her

Mariel Angus and Muriel at a peace rally, Ottawa, 2001

life's dedication to peace and justice. Visiting Muriel also challenged my perception of what it meant to be elderly. Her personality was so alive and engaging that it was hard to think of her as being in her nineties! I spent years when I was growing up hearing stories about her and the work she did from many of my family members, so I was glad to have had those afternoons to get to know her on a more personal level.

What I find most inspiring about Muriel's life was that, for all her awards and accolades, she was also in many ways a very ordinary person. She worked, raised a family and participated in her community. But it was her deep concern for social injustice, coupled with her ability to create deep and lasting relationships with people from many different walks of life, that made her extraordinary.

The diversity of people that Muriel touched in her life was reflected in those who attended her memorials. In both Montreal and Halifax, friends and family spoke of many aspects of her life — her active pacifism, her work as a feminist and her role as friend and mentor — with a great deal of thoughtfulness. While I regret not having more opportunities to be with her, hearing so much of other people's experiences of her made me feel that I came to know her better even in her passing. Her ability to inspire and challenge the many people she knew was evident in the words spoken by those at the memorials, and it was clear that her spirit and her passion for justice will live on in the many people whose lives she touched.

Our society has changed a great deal since Muriel was my age. I can't help wondering what it would have been like to grow up female in our society today if it hadn't been for pioneers like Muriel who paved the way for the creation of greater equality for women. I am thankful both for the work she did in helping create a society where women have more opportunities and for the example she set in doing so of how to be an engaged, active citizen. I feel honoured to have been named after someone who has had such a positive influence on so many people and on creating a more just society.

Ode to Muriel

Colleen Ashworth, Halifax

(*Written on the occasion of Muriel's ninetieth birthday, October 31, 1998*)

She is, quite simply, peace personified. A magnificent melange of qualities perfectly melded into a powerful presence.

Peace and power

peaceful power

powerful peace

Oxymorons? I think not — for together in her they provide a symbol of strength and serenity, of commitment and compassion, of knowledge and nurturing.

She has been honoured by many — formal awards, acknowledging her contribution to world peace, and the informal gratitude of many of us who have felt her subtle but profound influence.

I first experienced her when I was only eleven. Even then, in my childish version of the world, I knew that she was unusual (spiritual, I might have said, had I known that word).

Part of my insight came from others — from my mother's set, who found her odd — a type of woman they had never encountered at their bridge tables or afternoon tea parties:

She, they reported, spoke up in public and had opinions
on matters better left to the men;
She questioned the school system and presented her views
at home and school meetings, when she ought to have been
in the kitchen preparing the "eats."

My response to these tidbits of talk was one of rather confused admiration — even at that tender age I didn't fancy myself in the kitchen, but I also couldn't imagine ever being bold enough to speak out like she did.

My personal knowledge of her was on a different level, as mother of my good friend, Eleanor. I was often invited to their home and found myself inspired by the dynamic activity and joy which was displayed there. There was always animated discussion which seemed to encompass topics that were unknown to me in my home. Not that my own home life was unhappy, but it seemed to have a very narrow focus. Even in those teen years I had a vague longing to move beyond the boundaries which defined my life. And so in those early days a seed was planted, one which I assuredly did not comprehend at the time, but which has emerged and blossomed in my life.

Many years have passed since those first inklings of unrest, and many of my adventures and life experiences are a direct result of Muriel's interventions. In some ways, my whole sense of direction (when I can locate it!) has flowed from those early hours spent with the Duckworths. Her role in my life has been one of providing a model, a symbol of the qualities which are in all of us, but which are only fully manifested in some special lives. My aspirations to emulate her have never been fully realized, but she has given me the vision of how it could be done. And, for that, I am very grateful.

Remembering Our Muriel Duckworth

Marie Hammond-Callaghan, Sackville, N.B.

I first met Muriel in the early 1990s in Kay Macpherson's living room on Boswell Avenue in Toronto. As Kay's sight had been failing due to cataracts, she had invited me to read old letters and day books to her while she worked on her autobiography, *When in Doubt, Do Both: The Times of My Life* (1994). It was a memorable and delightful experience, giving me a whole new perspective on women's history. At that time I was in my late twenties and a relatively new member of the Toronto branch of the Voice of Women. I recall being so thrilled and honoured to become acquainted with one of Kay's best friends and co-activists. What attracted me most to the Voices was their indomitable, cheeky spirit, "speaking truth to power"; women who believed they could make a difference in a world where war always seemed to be a first resort. They were active citizens well into their seventies, eighties and nineties. I wanted to *be* them when I reached that age.

When I decided to move "back east" following my master's degree at OISE, a vigorous feminist community awaited me in the Halifax VOW. It was 1992, and we were still reeling from the devastation of the Gulf War. Although I was saddened to leave the Toronto VOW, Muriel and the wonderful group of women surrounding her welcomed me and made me feel I really belonged. It was like coming home even though I had never actually lived in Halifax. Pretty soon VOW activities absorbed much of my time — from contributing to the Atlantic VOW newsletter and preparing briefs, to organizing and attending regular meetings, often in the form of potlucks! Muriel's vision and energy were a powerful inspiration. My spouse, Kevin, once remarked (with a twinkle in his eye) that he was jealous of Muriel because I never said "no" to her.

What I remember most about Muriel was her warmth, generosity and unbounded interest in people. She took every person very seriously, made them feel included, made them feel they mattered. And she was open to all generations. This was perhaps part of what made her so intellectually curious. I was so impressed by the fact that her livingroom table was always covered with the latest political and social commentaries or scholarly journals. You could also expect her to draw new visitors to VOW meetings from a wide range of backgrounds and ages. I recall once how she invited a young twenty-year-old woman from a downtown coffee shop. But that was her way. Everyone I knew loved this about her. She was peace personified, our Muriel. She lived it. She used to quote A.J. Muste: "There is no way to peace, peace is the way."

Muriel had a deep soul. Her pacifism and Quaker views were also strongly informed by her feminism, socialism and overall dedication to human rights. Reflecting on how VOW always strove to dialogue with women from so-called "enemy" nations, she stressed, "Women in the world are not our enemies and we aren't going to behave as if they are." Muriel also believed women's experiences as mothers — the socially as-signed caregivers — gave women a special perspective on issues of war and peace. Indeed these were the origins of the VOW during the Cold War. She pointed out that the "Voice of Women was started in Canada in 1960 because there was a feeling that women's voices should be heard and there would be a difference in what women had to say about nuclear testing." As the VOW evolved over several decades, Muriel and other Voices became active in many campaigns, including protesting against the Vietnam War, supporting the rights of First Nations women and advocating for action on the United Nations Security Council Resolution 1325. The broad and rich scope of their focus on peace continued to attract a wide variety of women, including myself in the mid-1980s, when I became a VOW member at the tender age of twenty-five.

As it was for so many, VOW became my other university, the centre of my activist education. One of my most formative learning experiences was the VOW United Nations study tour in Vienna and Geneva, where I travelled in a group of ten politically seasoned members to network with other women's groups as well as lobby government representatives on issues of equality, peace and disarmament. However, another VOW experience had a truly transforming effect on me: my work for the Nova Scotia VOW investigating the impact of low-level military flights on Innu women and children in Labrador. The meaning of peace took on new dimensions for me as I visited the Innu community of Sheshashit with Halifax VOW member Betty Peterson and encountered strong Innu leaders

Berit Ås, a feminist academic and politician on speaking tour from Norway, Linda Christianson-Ruffman, Muriel and Marie Hammond-Callaghan, 1997

such as Elizabeth Penashue. These VOW experiences became a powerful inspiration, not only of my own feminist peace activism but also in my later academic scholarship on women's peace movements in Northern Ireland and Canada.

Muriel's impact on my life was profound. Indeed, knowing her may have been the greatest single reason I turned to feminist peace studies as my life's work. Also, I wanted to share Muriel with everyone I knew, especially my students in women's studies and history at Mount Allison University. One of the greatest recent memories I have of her was the rap song she did in 2004 when she came to Mount Allison to give the International Women's Day address. My students just fell in love with her. As the recipient of an honorary doctorate degree that year (her ninth I believe), Muriel gave an incredibly moving address on her pacifism at the Mount Allison convocation.

Although we have been deprived of her great presence, Muriel's rich vision and warm spirit continue to live on in our precious memories as well as in our own efforts to build a peaceful world.

Remembering Muriel

Margaret Murphy, Duncan Falls, B.C.

In the fall of 2003 I was deeply involved in the research and writing of a story of the life and times of Canadian poet E. Pauline Johnson. One evening, I glanced through my Women's Daybook, with its photos of outstanding women. There on the page looking back at me was the thoughtful face of Muriel Duckworth. I did not know her, nor did I recognize her name. But in an instant, I knew I needed to know more about this woman. The following week, around Muriel's ninety-sixth birthday, CBC TV carried a brief news item about the "relentless" Canadian peace activist. "There she is again," I said looking at her face. When Muriel's picture appeared in the *Vancouver Sun* a few days later, I knew I had to do something.

It was remarkably easy. Muriel lived in Halifax. I called information and was promptly given her telephone number on Bayers Road. I called her. Muriel Duckworth answered her phone. She was gracious, present and interested in this woman calling from the other side of the country. "Well," I stammered, "I'm a storyteller… and I know you don't know me… and I know we've never met… but I need to share your story. Would you agree to that?" Muriel laughed quietly. After a slight pause she said: "Do you really think people will want to hear it?" "Yes," I said, "everyone needs to hear it, especially now." I held my breath. More gentle laughter from Muriel. "Well, how could I say no to that!" she said.

"Thank you," I said, "thank you." I hung up the phone, both elated and anxious. And my head said: "Now, how on earth are you going to do this?"

Over the next few months my focus was on Pauline Johnson and preparing to share her story in Ontario. I called Muriel a few more times and she invited me to the cottage in Austin, Quebec. I was thrilled to be asked. I was going to the lake, that peaceful sanctuary where Muriel replenishes and restores her spirit every summer. I too love cottages, especially old cottages, with porches and fireplaces and long winding paths to the water. This was "Maple Crest," Muriel's family cottage. By 11:30 p.m. I would start to fade, the excitement of my days wrapping around me. But Muriel was still full of energy and light, taking phone calls as I wished her goodnight.

When I was leaving, I hugged her goodbye, and she said "Come again." I wept as I left, wondering yet again, how in the world would I capture her story and share parts of her life! Meeting Muriel is like receiving a torch and agreeing to carry it. There is energy shared and exchanged. No glory or bravado,

Muriel with Margaret Murphy, 2008

no fame or attention, but the strong irrefutable knowing of getting the job done. And I did. And my thanks are for Muriel, then and always.

Muriel with Erika and Helena Whyte, her great granddaughters,
at the Belleville family 100th birthday party

Muriel with grand-
daughter Sylvia at
the birthday party

Muriel eating
birthday cake with
grandson Nick
Schirmer at the
birthday party

Family Memories of Muriel

Anyone who visited Muriel either at her beloved Maple Crest cottage at Austin or in her apartment in Halifax would soon be invited to look at pictures of her children, her grandchildren and her latest great-grandchildren. No subject was dearer to her heart. In the same spirit, family members from two generations share with us some of their favourite memories of her.

Grandchildren's Testaments
Relayed by Sylvia, Martin's daughter, at the Montreal Memorial

From Anana Rydvald: I will always remember the trip Granny and I took on the train back to Halifax about five years ago. Someone working on the train knew about granny and was *very* honoured to have her on the train. We had a cabin at one end of the train and the dining area was at the completely opposite end, I expressed concern about this but he assured me that we should have our dinner first since we were taking off in the evening and once Muriel Duckworth was done to let him know and he would take care of things. After dinner I went up to him and said she was ready to go back to her cabin and expected him to get someone to help us walk back, but instead he said "sit back and relax." At the next station, he had someone waiting with a wheelchair who had Granny get off and sit in it, and then they *moved* the train for *her*. I didn't see anyone else around. I guess he had made a special request to do this just for her. I was very moved when I saw the train pass by with Granny sitting there and being a little "worried" about the train leaving! And when it stopped for her she was so humbled and polite as usual.

Love her and miss her. This was one of the best trips of my life. It felt like I was talking to a girlfriend, I could tell her anything. A great feeling for me since I didn't grow up with her, she really made me feel welcomed and loved.

From Anna Duckworth: I was sitting with her in her apartment this winter/spring and asked her what she thought of God. Did she believe? I told her I couldn't believe how silly and violent people were because of religion. She said (roughly): "I'll tell you what I think, dear. God is love and love is God, and that's about as far as I need to go with it."

It occurred to me then, she really was a wise diplomat. And that's what made her so universally appealing and loved (by most, anyway). I mean, really, how could any religion-crazed person be angry at her for saying that? What she said was pure goodness, but what she meant was: "Those people are *nuts!*"

But yikes! When I write that down, it occurs to me that it may offend people. It's 2009. Lighten up folks! Love, Anna.

Jackie Schirmer, Muriel's granddaughter, with niece Jean at Muriel's 95th birthday party

From Tiffany Duckworth: What has always warmed the cockles of my heart about Granny was her detailed knowledge of her ancestors and extended family and her constant effort to keep in touch with anyone in the family line. It has always made me feel like I was a part of something bigger and knew that I had a place (a bunch of places) to go if I felt alone. Love, Tiff.

Muriel with granddaughter Marya

From Danielle Schirmer: I have so many good memories of Granny ... especially from the cottage ... where her granola and fresh fruit greeted us in the morning; where she would wave to us from the porch as we swam in the lake; where her stories and company by the fire, along with a good game of crazy eights and hot chocolate, would entertain us on chilly evenings ... Bouquets of wildflowers, old knit sweaters, hummingbird feeder, squeeky swing, stars and sky ... She cared for her grandchildren in so many subtle ways.

My last memory of Granny is of visiting her in the hospital this summer. She must have been in so much pain having had a broken leg that wasn't yet immobile, but she hardly showed it. She and my daughter Sadie shared some fruit salad and tried on cousin Judy's bracelets together. She truly wanted to spend some quality time with her. She didn't let the pain keep her from enjoying the moment and the time she had with us. Even in this brief visit, she taught and gave me so much. I — we — will miss her.

From Marya Duckworth: My memories of Granny are forever melded with my memories of the cottage: watching her make tapioca pudding in the kitchen or angel food cake from scratch; calling the children up from the lake for lunch from the veranda with her trademark yodel; patiently helping a child with a jigsaw puzzle or playing a game of cards in front of the fireplace; napping on the chaise lounge by the living room window while listening to CBC radio.

My last memories of Granny are of watching her hold court from her hospital bed in Sherbrooke. She would ask a young doctor who just took her history what time the interview would air on TV. She would start a committee among those in her room and appoint a secretary to take minutes. My very last memory of Granny is when I spoke to her on the telephone three days before she died. I will never forget her last words. She told me that she loved me, and to take care.

From Sylvia Duckworth: What I loved most about granny was that she was so unassuming. One would never guess her social activist side unless one started talking to her about the issues she felt so passionately about. I don't remember her ever lecturing her grandchildren about the many injustices in the world. She was in all regards just a normal, loving grandmother who loved to spend time with her family. It always came as a surprise to me each time she won an honorary doctorate (ten, I think?) or would be profiled in a newspaper article because I never viewed her as an ardent feminist or pacifist: she was just my grandmother. And in her modesty, she was probably more surprised than anyone with all of the accolades she received over the course of her life.

Martin Duckworth, Muriel's son

During one of my visits to Mother during her last year, I went with her to a Friends meeting in Halifax. They had decided to stay together for a brief while after this meeting to discus their religious beliefs. They went around the circle, each one saying his/hers. When it came to Mother's turn, she said, very quietly: "I don't have any religious beliefs. I only have memories of extraordinary things:

"A baby's smile. I look at Sadie's picture every day [at that time her youngest great-grandchild] and wonder how is such a miracle possible?

"Handel's *Messiah*. When I was ten, we had a new minister at our church in Magog, and his wife was a soprano. They managed to produce a performance of *Messiah*.

"Discovering in the Student Christian Movement at McGill that there was not just one point of view that was right. Others' points of view could be as valuable as your own, and you could learn from them. That's how my daughter teaches.

"Discovering when I was working with teenaged girls in Hell's Kitchen, Lower East Side, New York, that mothers and daughters in conflict would

Muriel with son Martin and granddaughter Danielle Schirmer at her 100th birthday party

listen to each other if they were asked to change roles. There are those memories. I don't have religious beliefs."

In late July, about three weeks before Mum died, we arranged for a medical van to take her from her hospital bed in Magog to her beloved cottage in Austin for an afternoon visit. It was gorgeous day. Mum sat in her wheelchair on the porch, watching her grandson Nicholas and his girlfriend frolicking in the lake down below. When tea-time came, we asked Mum if she could do what she had always done when playtime was over, and that was to call the young ones up the hill with her eternal "Yoo-hoo!" She did it with enthusiasm and joy and didn't stop until the two young ones were up the hill and on the porch. Those were the last of a lifetime of "yoo-hoos." They started when I was playing on the street in NDG as a toddler. I still hear them. And I think they will always stay with me as Mum's eternal call to life.

Eleanor Duckworth, Muriel's daughter

Mum was so good at getting people talking. Any kind of group.

For the last six or eight years, her nieces made a point of assembling at the cottage, annually, for a few days — Kay Summers, Ruth Plumpton, Judy DeFusco, Jean Cooper. (Louella was too far away.) And I would be there, and once in a while, Audrey. One time, we had a few other women join us for dinner — Mum's cousin Melanie Black, and a neighbour or two. At a lull in the conversation (which hadn't quite found its way yet), she asked, "What do you remember about your first bathing suit?" I don't remember how the conversation went, but it really got going!

Eleanor with Muriel at the cottage, 2008

Another time, it didn't quite get to happen. For her last many years, Mum didn't have a doctor in Magog. For any medical care, she had to go to the emergency room, or to a specialized clinic, and wait. One time, we set out for a visit to a clinic. We went in the morning, and took books and a picnic lunch. We talked. We read. People went in to the office; came out of the office; left. Other people arrived. On it went. We had our lunch. Over lunch, the idea came to her that she was missing a good occasion to get a group talking. There was a major obstacle — some were English speakers and some, French speakers. (And by then we certainly knew which were which.) We figured out how to handle that, and we had just about phrased our opening question (to get some discussion about the availability of doctors and what might be done about it) — we were about to call everyone to attention — when we were called in to the doctor. She much regretted missing that occasion by not having acted earlier!

On the other hand, in Halifax once — perhaps after her hip replacement — she managed to get a bed in a rehab hospital, which was not a given, even for folks who had nobody to care for them at home. The doctor came to see her, with a flock of interns on their rounds, and she seized the occasion from the start — telling them all how fortunate she felt to be in that fine rehab hospital and how shameful it was that this care was not easily available to all who needed it. I can still see their stunned expressions.

At the bicentenary ceremonies in her native village of Austin, she was asked to say a few words, which she did. But she realized later in the day that she had forgotten to say one thing that was very important to her. She had forgotten to mention Phoebe, Nicholas Austin's wife, who in her late forties made that long winter trek with him with six of their seven children, and pioneered with him, making a living on the land. Phoebe was not mentioned all day, and mentioning her had been one of Mum's major intentions. Back at her cottage, that evening, she shed tears about that.

It took a long time to think of herself as old. One day at the cottage she had invited some friends for tea. They were the children of a McGill friend of hers and Dad's with whom she had kept in touch after their parents died. Mum spent most cottage days out on the verandah, and she spent that morning out there. But it was a cool-ish day, so in preparation for them, she wanted to build a fire in the fireplace and have the tea indoors, because, she said, they were quite old, these friends she had invited. They were in their seventies, She was at the time ninety-five. (They chose to have the tea outside.)

I was impressed with how she retained her dignity in the last year or so, when there was so much she could not do for herself. So many personal matters had to be carried out by someone else. She simply did and let do what she knew needed to be done. No avoidance. No complaining. No shame. No self-pity. Thank yous — without profusion.

I loved her sense of humour. She laughed very wholeheartedly when scientists "voted" to decide whether Pluto was a planet. I wish I could remember more. During her first week at the Berkeley, Bedford, a few months before her hundredth birthday, I sent this message to family: "I just called Mum. She was having a wonderful conversation with her friend Andrea Curry, whom she hasn't see for about five years and who is in town from Cape Breton. Andrea phoned Mum's Halifax number, and lo and behold, found Mum in this new place. At 10 a.m. Mum had gone to the exercise class, which she had found to be *just* what she wanted/ needed. Then she went outside by herself for a walk. She came in happily exhausted and just sat in the communal living room until it was time for lunch. "Life couldn't have been better." Her health was extraordinary. She had all (or perhaps almost all) her own teeth until her last six months. Her hearing was as good as ever, right to the end. In the month of her ninety-ninth birthday, I sent this message to a friend: "Mum saw her primary care physician today, after a long summer. The doctor cleared out her ear, which was itchy. All else was fine!"

I had the privilege of being with my mother this summer for all but two weeks. There were other helpers there all the time, as well. Always at least two people available — to care for her and for each other. In and around all the complications of hospital care-giving, we opened cards and notes that folks kept sending, we looked at photos, we read to her, we talked about our work, we rolled her around the corridor, we looked out the window, we watched the moon, we listened to music.

She was good company, as ever. She was brave, responsive, generous, concerned for everybody else, battling, guarding her sense of humour, guarding her spirit, guarding her passion for life, for living. She always knew who was with her — our names and who we were to her, and what to ask about our lives. She let us know wistfully that she would like to get back to the cottage at least one time before going back to Halifax. And we did manage to do that one day, with Martin, Audrey, Sylvia, Nick and a friend of his.

John, Martin and I were all with her the last few days. It was wonderful to be with her. To the end, she remained loving, humorous, generous, appreciative — and endlessly loveable.

John Duckworth, Muriel's son

Dad used to call Mum, "Meemo." (That is what her younger sister, Mildred, had called her.) I carried that tradition on now and then. She liked that.

We moved to Halifax after the war. The principal in the brand new Cornwallis Junior High School was a retired Army colonel. I was in the first ever grade seven in that school. Upon the opening of the school, the principal required all the boy students to participate in a cadet corps. When I came home and told Mum, she put down whatever she was working on, marched me back to the school and demanded a meeting with the principal. She made it very clear to him that there was no way her son was going to be forced into participating in anything of a military nature. I ended up playing basketball while the rest carried out their weekly drills.

When Mum was about seventy years old, brother Martin was premiering a film he made about the Cape Breton coal miners' strike. The premier was in Glace Bay, N.S. Mum and Eleanor took the car from

Son John with his mother Muriel, 2006

Halifax, but since it was a gorgeous day, I couldn't resist taking my motorcycle. As our caravan drove to Cape Breton, Mum and Eleanor took turns driving the car and hanging on to me on back of the motorcycle. Very sporty ladies.

About the same time, there was a provincial election in Nova Scotia. The Conservatives had been in power forever. I wanted the Liberals to take over. When George Mitchell announced that he was going to run for the Liberals in my riding I called him right away to offer to help. We were well underway with George's campaign when Mum decided to run for the NDP in the same riding. This was somewhat of a dilemma, but I decided to keep working for George because I really wanted the Liberals to win the election and the NDP had no chance. I think they had one member in the House. So while I went door to door with George, Dad went door to door with Mum. To make matters even more bizarre, the Conservative candidate in the same riding was George Cooper, and Claudia, my wife at the time, was spending a lot of time helping George's pregnant wife, Cynthia, get ready to deliver her first child. I have never heard of a more incestuous three-party election situation. Mum did not win that election, but she accomplished what she set out to do — raise and discuss important issues and prepare the way for more women to run in subsequent elections.

When Mum and Dad were living in New York City in 1929, someone gave them tickets to see the Metropolitan Opera. Mum was overwhelmed by the grandeur of the place and the performance. She faithfully listened to every Saturday afternoon live performance on the radio, and she knew many of the operas very well. When the old Met was torn down and the fundraising started for the new Met, I bought Mum a special box collection of Met Opening Nights on LPs. In the box came a two-square-inch portion of the stage curtain of the old Met. Mum cherished it and kept it until her granddaughter, my daughter Samantha, got married. At that point Samantha was playing contra bassoon in the Metropolitan Opera orchestra. Mum thought that Samantha should have that piece of memorabilia, so my wife, Anne Fouillard, had it framed, and Mum gave it to Samantha as a wedding gift.

When Mum was ninety-three, I decided to take her back to the Met. I called the ticket office and ordered tickets to two operas. While the seller was doing his thing, I mentioned to him that I was taking my mother to the Met and that the last time she was there was over seventy years ago. There was no reaction. Then after a couple of minutes he said, "That's what we like — repeat customers."

Taking Mum back to the Met was an amazing experience, made even more wonderful by her granddaughter playing in the orchestra. Being accustomed to seeing most of my entertainment on a television screen, I was completely overwhelmed by the opera house itself, let alone the singing, the orchestra, the acting, the incredible sets, trying to see the action and read the translation of the words on the back of the seat in front of me, trying to understand the story and trying to hear the contra bassoon. I was totally exhausted. But Mum just sat there calmly. She knew the story, she knew the music. She just seemed to be in heaven. We went to two different operas, *Tosca* and *The Marriage of Figaro*. We had a great time.

It was so great that Mum and Betty Petersen had each other. What an amazing pair of women. They were sisters-in-arms and both had such fun doing what they loved to do. Betty would drive Mum to all the unending social justice events and rallies and they would do post mortems on the way home. They lived in my house on Coburg Road (it became known as The Quaker House) for several years together with a number of students, including Marion Keran's daughter, Joanne Kelllerman, and Elizabeth May, who were both Dalhousie law students at the time, Sylvie Pelletier and two Nigerian men, who were also Dal students. I was living and working in New England at that time, but would return home now and then and keep the furnace company in the basement. It was on those brief visits to that communal home, when I was about forty years old, that I really saw Mum for the first time as someone other than my mother. I observed her ability to deal with people and situations and started to understand what it was about her that made her so unique, so successful at turning ideas into reality and so loved. I became her greatest admirer and loved her easygoing and pleasant company.

Mum would often come to our house in Kingsburg for Christmas. One year, Eleanor was driving her from Halifax after dark on a cold Christmas Eve. We knew that there could be black ice on the back road to our house. Anne felt that something was wrong when they did not turn up when they should have. Then the phone rang. It was the hospital in Lunenburg. The car had slipped on the ice and rolled upside down into a big ditch. Eleanor and Mum were both wearing seat belts, which meant they were both hanging upsidedown in the car in the ditch. A woman who was a reporter from the local weekly newspaper happened to be in the first car to discover them. They were released from their unusual positions, strapped to emergency board stretchers and taken to the hospital for checking. They were released shortly after and were both in good shape. There was an article in the paper the next week by that reporter. It wasn't so much a news article, but more an account of the reporter's feelings on being the one who discovered the car in the ditch, at night, in the middle of the winter, with the two upsidedown women.

Food was a very important thing in Mum's life. Anne pointed out to me that every time we talked to Mum on the phone about what she had done, or where she had been the previous day, she would always tell us what food had been served. Whenever anyone came to visit her, she would have food and/or drinks out right away. When she was in her last years, if I was in her apartment when people came to visit, I would automatically get the juice and cookies out. She loved ice cream. In the morning she would talk about the need for her to diet, but she would never be able to resist having ice cream for dessert after dinner.

Mum never complained even when her arthritis was resulting in great pain. That is a very characteristic. She was always so appreciative of any little thing you did for her that you would want to do more and more for her.

When her personal physical and medical needs became too great and she really could not continue to live by herself anymore, she decided that she did not want anyone to move in with her. So she moved from her apartment to the Berkeley in Bedford. It is an apartment building but with a dining room and a full-time nursing and caregiving staff. She loved the Berkeley and the staff and they loved her. She never tired of the view of the ocean from the chair where she sat. It was here where I noticed that many of the other residents seemed to be living lonely lives. Mum, on the other hand, had a constant stream of visitors, the result of a long lifetime of involvement in her many causes and the hundreds of close friendships that she made and nourished. Although all her contemporaries had passed away, she just kept on accumulating more and more friends and admirers of all ages.

Every summer, Mum would go back to the place where she was born — Austin, Quebec. She was the oldest known living descendant of Nicholas Austin, the New Hampshire Quaker who settled in this part of Quebec at the time of the American Revolution. Sometime around 1995, the Town of Austin decided to celebrate the two hundredth anniversary of the arrival of Nicholas Austin. The organizers contacted Mum to see whether she would participate. She agreed, and on the day of the celebration, Mum and Anne and our two daughters, Anna and Alex, and I sat in an old cart and were pulled along Austin's dirt road by a pair of oxen. Along the side of the cart was a big banner saying "The Descendants." There were about a hundred spectators lined up along the dirt road, and as we were pulled along at a speed of about a mile a day, we waved at these hordes. It seemed like we waved at each person for about fifteen minutes.

After Dad died, Mum would take the train up to Austin, and one of the family members would accompany her each way. Later on, she found the train too difficult, and I started to drive her there in June and back home in September. The trip would always take two days. In her last years, Mum would have a hard time getting in and out of the car and really could not go up stairs. So when she needed to go to the bathroom, it would always be fun trying to find the perfect circumstances. We had to find a public bathroom, on the ground floor, with no stairs, where there were no other users. Tim Horton's was out of the question. We usually found a hotel. Then I would open the trunk and get out the elevated toilet seat in its big box and the walker. I would assemble the walker and Mum would extricate herself from the car and walk with her walker to the hotel. Then she would wait outside the ladies room while I looked both ways to make sure no one was looking. Then I would go in and assemble the elevated toilet seat on top of toilet. Then I would open the door and let Mum in. I would wait outside the ladies room door until she called from inside that she was ready to have me come in and help her get up off the toilet. I would help her up to her walker, disassemble and box the elevated toilet seat, open the washroom door from the inside and Mum would walk out with her walker to the car. I would follow, disassemble the walker and help Mum into the car. And off we would go. Where I was used to two-minute pit stops of this nature, these would take a half an hour, but each time was so memorable that I can point out every washroom we visited together from here to Quebec.

Mum was a very emotional person. She was regularly moved to tears when she tried to tell people about incidents that moved her. I inherited that gene in spades.

The NDP finally came to power in Nova Scotia for the first time in 2009. Mum, who was then a hundred years old, went to the public swearing-in ceremony of the new cabinet at the Cunard Centre on the Halifax waterfront. When Darrell Dexter was sworn in as premier, silent tears started to roll down Mum's face.

One of the first things Darrell Dexter wanted to do as premier was acknowledge Mum as the first woman to ever run as a candidate for the NDP in Nova Scotia and as the oldest and most active NDP supporter in the province. It was decided that she should be awarded the Order of Nova Scotia. By this time however, Mum was in the hospital in Magog, Quebec, having fallen and broken her leg just a few days after arriving at her cottage for the summer of 2009. Premier Dexter wanted to bestow the Order on Muriel in person and advised us that he was prepared to go to Magog to do so. Before the arrangements could be made, however,

Mum contracted pneumonia, and the resulting antibiotics more or less did her in. Premier Dexter called Mum on the telephone. Martin, Eleanor, Audrey, Anne and I were in the room. I held the phone to Mum's ear, and the premier talked to her and thanked her for all the amazing things she had accomplished. He told her she had done Nova Scotia, Canada and the world a great service and he informed her that she had been awarded Nova Scotia's highest honour. She was unable to acknowledge his remarks verbally, but we are sure she heard him thank her for her years of tireless effort promoting peace, women's rights and social justice.

I asked Mum what she thought would happen to her when she died. She said that she wanted her body to be cremated, but that she hoped her spirit and soul would live on in the people she had met while she lived. I am sure this hope will come to pass.

Audrey Schirmer, Muriel's daughter-in-law

I first met Muriel in April of 1971. My sister, Abbie, and I were going to meet the "Viet Cong women" — women who travelled to Toronto to meet with Canadian and American women to tell them about the Vietnam War. Some walked through the jungle for six months in order to be able fly out of Vietnam for these meetings. We lived in Cambridge, Massachusetts, at the time, and my sister, a teacher, was bringing school books to be shipped to Cuba. We met a woman in the Montreal airport, on our way to Toronto, who would take care of getting them to the right place. Her name was Eleanor Duckworth.

We got to the Toronto airport at the same time as the Vietnamese women and were invited to take the bus with them to the conference. On that bus

Muriel with her daughter-in-law Audrey Schirmer, 2007

was Muriel Duckworth. Getting off that bus the women were greeted by a gentleman named Jack Duckworth. The conference began that evening in a big hall at OISE. I was taking pictures at that time for a Journal called *Clergy and Laity Concerned*. There was a man filming as well. At the end of the evening, I asked that man if he knew of a darkroom so I could get my pictures developed as soon as possible. He said he was staying at a place with a darkroom. That man was Martin Duckworth. We fell madly in love, just after I had sworn off all men! Abbie and I helped him film the rest of conference. Abbie did sound and I, in between picture-taking, held up his pants that were otherwise continually slipping down.

We had a great time. The Vietnamese women were courageous and kind. They talked little about their families; they had not much time to spend with them during that war! It was a wonderful way to meet Muriel and Jack. I will never forget it. And Muriel, I learned much later, was one of the Canadian women responsible for making it happen! She was a doer, devoted to peace in the world, and a friend to many, and I am lucky to be one of the many.

Ruth Plumpton, Muriel's niece

I'm Ruth Plumpton, the elder daughter of Muriel's sister Mildred. For two years in the late 1940s, Muriel and her family looked after my sister Jean and me when our mother became ill and was not able to care for us. That bond stayed with us for a lifetime.

To the end of her life, Muriel was always aware of what all of the members of her extended family were up to. She enjoyed getting letters and phone calls with news of even the young-

Ruth Plumpton and Muriel in Lake Memphremagog, celebrating her last trek down to her beloved lake, July 2005

est great grandnieces and nephews. In the last year of her life, when she was unable to make the calls herself, she had each of her children call to enquire about an ill family member. If I ever assumed that she was too busy to chat, she'd correct me and say she loved getting my calls. However, once when she was in her early nineties, she did say, "You'll have to call me back later dear. We're having a meeting about holding effective meetings." So I knew that she never lost her commitment to all of the social justice causes she had dedicated her life to supporting.

In fact, what struck me the most as she went through her nineties was Muriel's continuing strong engagement with the world, particularly her commitment to the search for peaceful solutions. She cared about peace and social justice at every level, even the personal. It appeared to me that many people relied on her good judgment to help them with personal issues long past the time when one would think she'd be so engaged. She really could listen and get people to talk about themselves. There was no problem too small to attract her caring attention. The telephone allowed her to keep abreast of all that went on in the outer world and the world of family and friends. She kept it within reach at all times. Her strong telephone voice seemed to belong to someone in her sixties. Her ability to stay engaged and not despair was an inspiration. I think that's one factor that allowed her to be independent for so long.

Muriel loved her summers at her cottage on Lake Memphremagog in Quebec to the end of her life. Even though it was frequently busy there, she said it was a wonderful time to recharge her batteries and have some time for reflection. We all visited her there when we could over the years. In her late nineties, she was good at taking naps and letting us look after physical details, but she was wonderful company and encouraged us all to enjoy the sun and lake.

The summer of her hundredth year, Muriel celebrated at the cottage with over eighty family and friends. Then she travelled to Belleville to the home of her niece, Kay Summers, for another big party of family and friends. This was all before the wonderful formal recognition in Halifax in October 2008. It was so special to be there and see the affection and respect from her friends in Nova Scotia for all that she had contributed to that community. Even that event had a social justice purpose. Not many people get to be feted in this way during their lifetime. Muriel deserved it. I still miss her.

Jean Cooper, Muriel's niece

I am Jean Cooper, the younger daughter of Muriel's sister Mildred. Although my sister, Ruth, and I saw Auntie Muriel over the years, we have special memories of her last twelve years because of our annual visits to her cottage (commonly known as "the cottage").

When my sister retired, we decided to visit Auntie Muriel for a few days in July at the cottage. We also thought that we would be helpful in being there and giving others a day or two off. Of course, in true Muriel fashion, she arranged that we wouldn't be the only two visiting at that

Front: Muriel and Jean Cooper (neice), back row: Kay Summers (niece), Audrey Schrimer (daughter in law), Judy DeFusco (niece), Eleanor (daughter), Ruth Plumpton (niece), 2002

time. Our annual trek became the cousins' visit. This was usually limited to the cousins of the older generation, that is, the daughters and sons of her siblings and herself.

She continued to be the gatherer of people, giving us the gift of her memory and time. She never lost her appetite for discovery or growth. We shall remember the lovely lavender fields on the east side of Lake Memphremagog; the sunsets at the top of the hill to Austin; the almost-competitive visit we made to one of her older friends, when we all descended to the shores of the lake for a swim on a very cold day. Ruth and I certainly wouldn't have swum that day if it hadn't been for the two ladies in their nineties already in the water. Even when recovering from one of her fractures, she welcomed our visits, dutifully did her exercises, scolded us about working so hard on the grounds and encouraged us to have the swims in the lake that we loved so much.

The yearly pictures from those visits show a woman aging much more slowly than one would expect. Lots of smiles all around. Of course, the last year's visit meant that Muriel was in the hospital, but even there she took great interest in all the staff and fellow patients, again focusing on others. To live a life so full of interest, love and generosity is something she achieved. Thanks, Auntie Muriel, Jean

Eulogies for Muriel from across the Country

Finally, I selected for our bouquet a few of the eulogies made by friends at the memorials held across Canada which reflect Muriel's love of life, of peace, of justice, of education, of feminism and of all humanity.

From Austin, Quebec

Anne Wonham

I am one of the lucky people of Austin who counted Muriel as a friend. J'ai eu la chance d'être une voisine et amie de Muriel, this woman of passion and of peace, who would have been so pleased to see you all here this afternoon...

Her remarkable accomplishments and accolades are well documented on the web, où, d'après La Tribune, une recherche Google donne plus de résultats pour Muriel Duckworth que pour Jean Charest. It was not, however, this public persona that I knew, but a neighbour, a dedicated Austinoise, born on Halloween in 1908 on the kitchen table in what is now Le Hameau near Bryant's Landing, and schooled in the one-room school house by the creek. Muriel always claimed that she owed her good health to the immunity she acquired from that school's drinking water, which was served to the children from a common cup dipped into a pail.

Elle était très fière d'être une descendante de Nicholas Austin, et de son épouse si souvent oubliée, que Muriel appelait "Poor Phoebe." To her delight during the Austin bicentennial in 1993, Muriel and some of her immediate family, all direct descendants of first settlers Nicholas and Phoebe Austin, were pulled in a cart through the streets of Austin by a pair of oxen. She loved our Austin community, and always made an effort to participate in local events and to support local initiatives.

The woman I knew was a woman of contrasts. She had a formidable intelligence, but never tried to one-up anyone. She was an ardent feminist who enjoyed the company of men. It was all right to have her cottage so full of visitors that someone had to sleep on a mattress in the bathroom, but she always insisted that everyone sit down to three meals a day at a properly set table.

Muriel had many interests in addition to her lifelong commitment to the planet, the poor, the disenfranchised, the victims. For example:

A love of the natural world. Each year on the Summer Solstice, June 21, she would stay outside as much as possible in order to revel in the longest day of the year. Wildflowers were on her table and humming birds at her feeders, and even in her latter years, she was always game to be driven down to Bryant's Landing to watch the moon rise over her beloved lake, or to the Catholic Cemetery to watch the sun set.

An appreciation of music and art. Every Saturday afternoon she would sit down by the radio to listen to the opera. On her walls are carefully chosen paintings alongside yellowing drawings done by small children. Both were admired and cherished. Even after she could no longer drive, she would take the bus in to Montreal to watch the Film Festival at the end of the summer.

La politique, l'actualité, les livres, les affaires; elle s'interessait a tout. Mais quelles étaient ses priorités personnelles? Je dirais qu'elles étaient les suivantes, pas nécessairement dans un ordre particulier:

1. To live in the moment, and to rejoice in it. Certainly there were great sorrows in her life, but these she did not dwell on, although she did always regret that she had never been arrested for being an activist. Her address book, its yellow cardboard covers held on with elastic bands, and full of old addresses, outdated numbers and obscure entries, was impenetrable to anyone else. But she could navigate through it, and would often call from Halifax just to say how beautiful the Atlantic Ocean looked from her win-

dow. Although Eleanor says that only a tiny strip was visible, if you hadn't answered the phone Muriel would leave a long message about the colour of the water and how happy she was that she could see it.

Muriel visited at the cottage by Professor Wonham and two of his exchange students from China

2. Always to ask the question: What can I do to make a bad situation better, whether it be an awkward social gathering or the threat of nuclear warfare?

3. Mais surtout elle s'intéressait aux gens. Above all she showed her love and concern for and loyalty to her family, her friends and her worldwide community. And friends she had. Muriel was a people magnet. Elle attirait les gens — comme le miel, les abeilles — peu importe leur age, leur métier, leur capacité ou leur nationalité.

Elle était l'amie de tous. There was a zone of serenity and tranquility around her that made people feel safe and valued, and there was joy and laughter in her conversations. She talked to you as though you were the most important and valuable person in the room, and as a result people wanted to be with her. Even strangers responded to her charm.

There is one more story to tell. A few years ago at a summer dinner the subject of personal goals arose. Others at the table listed professional ambitions, aspirations for their children or various forms of self improvement. Someone turned to Muriel, then in her mid-nineties, and asked somewhat in jest what *her* goals were. Without missing a beat she replied, "I want to keep spending my summers at the lake until I'm a hundred." Pause. Grin. "And then I'll reassess."

She reached that goal. She came to the lake as she had almost every summer for more than a century, and in her hundred and first year she reassessed.

Halifax Friends Memorial, August 3, 2009
Donna Smyth

When I think of Muriel, I think of circles. Many kinds of circles and how they are a perfect symbol for her and her work in the world.

For most of her adult life, Muriel advocated the kind of radical equality espoused by the early Quakers, who challenged the hierarchical structures of power in their society by simple acts. They sat together as friends, as equals, to worship in silence until moved to speak; they refused to doff their hats to those regarded as socially superior. Their audacity caused much trouble for them. Many early Quakers were beaten and/or put in jail by the authorities. Late in her own life one of Muriel's minor regrets was that she was never arrested for non-violent civil disobedience. She did, however, manage to stir up quite a lot of trouble.

Muriel came to Friends from a Protestant Social Gospel background. In 1962, Helen and Murray Cunningham gathered a small group of friends to sit together for worship. This was the genesis of the Halifax monthly meeting. Attracted by the Peace Testimony, Muriel and Jack sat with them. They were disillusioned with the United Church, whose moderator at that time refused to allow the Church to become involved with the growing anti-nuclear movement.

In 1975, after Jack died, Muriel became a formal member of the Meeting. This was not an easy decision for her as she did not consider herself a conventional Christian. All her life, she was a seeker: one who asked questions of others and herself. In the end, she believed that Jesus was a great teacher with a simple and profound message: Love one another.

Muriel practised this love in every aspect of her life. It was the motivation behind her work as a social activist fighting poverty and racism; advocating equality for women; struggling to put an end to war. It was behind her decision to withhold her taxes in the Conscience Canada Peace

Fund. It was the force behind her extraordinary presence, her ability to put people at ease and allow us to come out from behind our barricades to talk to her and to each other. She called forth the power of love from all of us, and often we surprised ourselves by what we could do with that power.

Muriel lived as she believed and often quoted Martin Luther: "Here I stand. I can do no other." Her convictions came from the heart and the mind. She was never one to check her mind at the door, and she never closed the door of her mind. One of the amazing things about her was her ability to learn and grow throughout her life. One thing morphed into another, like the circles spread in water when you toss a stone. Circles expanding outwards to embrace more and more of creation.

Muriel's two mantras in her final years were: War is stupid. God is Love. And she always came back to her favorite quotation from the poet Adrienne Rich (*The Dream of a Common Language*):

My heart is moved by all I cannot save
So much has been destroyed
I have to cast my lot with those who,
age after age, perversely,
with no extraordinary power,
reconstitute the world.

This speaks to us, dear Friends. We know that Muriel expects us to keep on reconstituting the world, one circle at a time. Carrying on, always carrying on.

Halifax Memorial, September 27, 2009
Gillian Thomas

For those of us who've learned some of the most important things we know from Muriel, "educator" seems like a too-formal and a too-inadequate word. She's been publicly honoured for her many years of work with such organizations as the Home and School Association and the Adult Education Division of the Nova Scotia Department of Education. But

Muriel receiving an honorary doctorate at Saint Mary's University, 2007

Muriel's approach to education was more complex and more passionate than institutional labels suggest.

Consider for a moment, the day eighty years ago when the young Muriel Ball received her McGill degree. Remembering that day many years later, she recalled that her feet ached from the previous night's graduation dance and that she was preoccupied with the thought of her marriage to Jack Duckworth two weeks hence. But she also recalled that in those years women graduating from McGill were each supposed to carry a dozen roses. Muriel discussed this with some of her friends and concluded that the custom imposed a real financial burden on some of their classmates. Therefore, they would all choose to break with tradition and do without.

That early action seems to have the real Muriel hallmark: The penetrating question that goes, very literally, to the heart of the matter. The shared insight. Followed by the action that it demands.

Muriel's questions were always remarkable, not only for their directness and originality but also for the undivided attention she could bring to the conversation. Education, for Muriel, was never about acquiring credentials, but always about gaining the knowledge, the wisdom and the skills that enabled advocacy. The world around her was her college without walls where all were teachers and all were students. She also saw education as an urgent collective project because she agreed with H.G. Wells that the future is "a race between education and catastrophe."

More than sixty years after receiving her degree from McGill Muriel addressed graduating students at Dalhousie Law School's convocation. She spoke about her work as an advocate for peace, for social justice and for education and concluded by quoting these words by Margaret Laurence:

> Your own life and work and friendships and love will come to an end, because one day you will die … but life and work and friendship and love will go on, in others, your inheritors. The struggle for peace and social justice will go on — provided that our earth survives and caring humans still live.

Halifax Memorial, September 27, 2009

Betty Peterson

Yes. Muriel was passionately against *war* in all its forms — the violence and the killing, the arms race, nuclear threats, nuclear subs in Halifax Harbour. She sought out the real causes of war: greed, power, injustice, poverty and the failure to find other ways to meet crises through negotiation and mediation.

She loved people and working with them for social change. If she was not always there in the forefront, she was always a leading light. When she could no longer march or leaflet at vigils, she came with her walker, and finally, in her nineties, she came and just sat! But she was there! She was dignified and eloquent, yet full of fun. But sometimes she was just a plain-speaking woman with her no-nonsense cry, "War is stupid!!!" She was also a great motivator, and when she got on that telephone and *you* we re called, you knew you'd better "git up and *go!*"

She was forthright and courageous on the streets and in high places, whether as a Raging Granny or as a Voice of Women for Peace.

But Muriel was even more concerned about working for peace in positive ways, not just against war. She spoke truth to power in Ottawa to change foreign policy, strongly supported women in politics and worked for international peace treaties at the United Nations and for promoting women in negotiating roles. During the Cold War she went to the Soviet Union as part of a Peace and Friendship delegation. And much more…

There were times when Muriel knew she had to be ready to stand alone and say, along with Martin Luther, "Here I stand. I can do no other." One of those times was when she refused to pay her taxes that went toward preparation for war. And the government was not pleased!

Muriel's source of strength was not only in working for peace, but in being peace, being centred and at peace within herself. As a Quaker, a member of the Religious Society of Friends, she affirmed their traditional Testimony Against War, any war, all war. She was a believer in Albert Schweitzer's Reverence for Life and in Gandhi's teachings on non-violence. She believed that pacifism does not mean passivism but that highly principled non-violent direct action and resistance is a tool to be used in conflict rather than weapons of war and mass destruction.

As Muriel has said, "My world view is the relationship between all things, and I believe that Love is my Guiding Light."

Dear Muriel, your Light still shines and the darkness cannot put it out.

Montreal Memorial, September 18, 2009

Bonnie Klein

My name is Bonnie Klein, and I got to know Muriel when Terre Nash and I made the NFB Studio D film *Speaking Our Peace: a Film about Women, Peace, and Power*. That was Muriel!

Thanks to Martin and to Michael for allowing me to be here with you to feel Muriel's presence among us one more time.

When Muriel died, I wrote Martin that his mother was the woman I wanted to be when I grow up. Me, Terre, Dorothy Henaut, Yael and how many hundreds of women of our generation in this room and across Canada. She was our elder and role model.

What are the qualities that spoke to us younger feminists so deeply? Muriel was not a "powerhouse" in today's careerist terms. She had no impressive credentials or even profession. She thought of herself as a very ordinary, down-to-earth woman. That was her credibility, her strength.

She did not wait for permission to speak truth to power. And therefore had extraordinary power.

Muriel's fierce anger at injustice was fuelled by love, love for women and for our male allies as well. When we spoke on the phone, she always asked for Michael and Seth. Muriel was inclusive at a time when some of us were not.

She modelled for us a life of inclusion and balance, where the personal and the political were constantly integrated. As one of her many best friends, Ursula Franklin, says, we write our letters to the editor and plan our demonstrations just like we do the dishes.

In Muriel and her wide network of conspirators — many of you here today, we who thought we were inventing feminism discovered that we were standing on the shoulders of wise and brave women who came before us. We came to understand that what we wanted as women was not a bigger piece of the pie, which was fundamentally rotten, but to change the recipe. (Cooking and eating were/are an important piece of our strategy.)

Many of you commented on this beautiful necklace of paper cranes I'm wearing.

On August 5, 1987, Michael and I were scheduled to join Muriel, Kay Macpherson and other friends to mark Hiroshima Day together and set paper lanterns on her beloved Lake Memphramagog. That turned out to be the day I had my stroke. Many weeks later, Muriel visited me, carrying a shoebox. In it were a thousand tiny paper cranes — you all know the story of Sadako. They were folded by Muriel's granddaughter, Martin and Audrey's daughter Danielle, who was then around twelve years old. Later, Danielle strung them into this necklace. It has hung on my bedpost, first in hospital and ever since, a talisman, a symbol of healing, a precious connection with Muriel.

On our last phone conversation, I told Muriel that our son Seth's daughter Zoe has always loved this necklace and the story behind it. It was one of the few things I wouldn't let Zoe play with as a baby. I told her that I loved it too much and it is very fragile — like life itself. Several months ago, when we were cuddling in my bed, five-year-old Zoe reached out to the necklace, touched it gently, and whispered, "Bubbe, Do you think I can have this necklace when you die?"

It is just one of the small links in the chain woven from Muriel and her family to me and my family, and one day hopefully to Zoe's. Many of you have Muriel stories like this. We are all part of that chain or circle of life, and we will continue. Muriel has not left us. May we all grow up to be like Muriel.

Montreal Memorial, September 18, 2009

Elaine Newman

I was brought up in Montreal. My mother and father were involved in Notre Dame de Grace community affairs and became friendly with Jack and Muriel, a relationship which I was fortunate to inherit. Eleanor and Martin and I went to grade school together. Here's a piece of our family folklore. When the "Y" exiled Jack to Halifax, they had trouble selling their NDG house. My mother was in advertising and rewrote the ad, including a couple of lines about family dinners in the kitchen and around the fireplace. It sold within a few days.

My husband Vijay Mathur and I toured Nova Scotia in 1971 in Muriel's mini minor. We fell in love with Nova Scotia, having already fallen in love with the Duckworths.

I have known many people who speak good ideas, but I don't know many who actually live them. It's easy to believe in peace but it isn't easy to refuse to pay the part of your taxes that supports the military. Or to leave a church in which you spent years of your life because they compromised on peace issues. Perhaps most extraordinary, though, was establishing the NDP in Nova Scotia, which seems nothing short of miraculous.

However, at a personal level, it was none of this that entranced me. It was the total honesty with which Muriel approached the world that I found amazing. Whenever I had a chance to talk with her, whatever we talked about, I had to think out carefully and thoroughly what I meant. She would join the discussion with the same care. There was no compulsion to agree — and I often didn't and still don't. But one had to think out the implications and say it straight. I found this exhilarating.

For instance, in my earlier years, I didn't care much about the death penalty. In conversations with Muriel, I tried to defend it and found I couldn't, and to this day, I oppose it. In this case, it was not a particular argument that Muriel made — it was a world view that I responded to.

I found it impossible to be less than honest with Muriel, and knowing her made me a better person. I am grateful for every minute I spent with her.

Vancouver Friends Meeting, September 26, 2009
Barbara Taylor

It was quite a day, and a lovely, sunny fall one, at that. We met at the Quaker/Friends Meeting House, on their lower level to be accessible to wheelchairs (Bonnie's) and walkers (quite a few). It followed a typical Quaker memorial meeting format: we sat in silent circle for a bit until the first person was moved to speak, and then almost everyone spoke of their affection and fond memories of Muriel.

At the end of the service, three of us Raging Grannies led the rest in singing a new version of "Women Shoulder Half the Burden," to the tune of "Coming through the Rye," revised for Muriel's memorial by Granny Molly Walsh of Montreal.

Women shoulder half the burden
Hold up half the sky.
Yet our voices have been muted
Makes you wonder why.

Muriel heard the voice of women
Calling you and me —
A peaceful world is one of justice
Love the golden key.

Muriel bravely faced the burden
Of humanity —
Marching, leading, teaching, speaking
Seeking harmony.

Her legacy to one and all
Now calls to you and me —
Help build a peaceful world of justice
Where love's the golden key.

With passion she took up each cause
And sought to find a cure.
Muriel was an inspiration…
Her spirit will endure.

Salt Spring Island, B.C.

Marion Pape

I recently helped to organize a memorial service for Muriel at the Vancouver Quaker Meeting Centre and listened to attendees talk about this remarkable woman. This short article has been informed by the love shown by the people who attended that memorial. And it is a reflection of how much she was loved from coast to coast to coast.

What is it about this woman, Muriel Duckworth, who has so captivated our hearts and minds? If the Canadian military in Afghanistan could figure out how to woo the hearts and minds of Afghans, we wouldn't have so much destruction, dead soldiers and massive expenditures. But that's the point, isn't it? War is not the answer, and Muriel steadfastly repeated that mantra over and over again.

I moved to Halifax in 1990 from the Northwest Territories where I was a remote member of the Canadian Voice of Women for Peace (VOW). Shortly after I arrived, I met a woman on a hiking outing who was a member of VOW and knew Muriel Duckworth well. The very next day, I received a call from Muriel asking all about me and inviting me to become involved with Halifax VOW. I became a member and have been ever since, in large part because I was so captivated by this woman.

One of the processes used by Nova Scotia VOW to review the health of the organization was to hold an annual retreat known as a Day of Renewal. Muriel was an important part of these renewals, bringing in key speakers who reminded us of the VOW's past as well as guiding us into the future. At these Days of Renewal, ideas were presented, reviewed, put into a practical context and then implemented — all by consensus. Everyone had an understanding of the importance of the work we were doing, the vision of what we wanted to accomplish and the confidence and support we would give and receive by working together.

Muriel was committed to the VOW and knew instinctively how to attract people to help the peace cause. But more importantly, perhaps, she loved meeting new people and knew how to connect them. She would start her conversation with a total stranger by saying: "Now dear, who are you? Tell me about yourself"; and then you become the focus of her universe. And after she gets to know you, Muriel never stops asking about you.

Muriel became involved and stayed involved as an activist throughout her whole life. She was a helpful mentor, offering sensibility and inspiration. There was that absolute commitment that inspired her in everything she did. One person at her memorial in Vancouver mentioned how activists so often burn out after putting their whole heart and soul into a cause. And then they spend the next thirty to forty years of their life being cynical and jaded, always complaining about how things are not working. Even in the face of everything going wrong, Muriel maintained positive activism throughout her whole life, inspiring people and fighting for peace and justice issues.

Another participant at the Vancouver memorial talked about Muriel's election campaign when she ran for the NDP in a Conservative Halifax riding. In the face of derision she would continually disarm her detractors by showing her concern for them to such an extent that, although she did not win, she got many votes from non-NDP supporters. She was one of those remarkable individuals who show that a single person can make an amazing difference.

Muriel had great wisdom and we all listened. She was active in many issues and organizations related to peace and social justice, and she brought us all together encouraging us to work both individually and collectively. She was spunky and didn't wait for permission; she knew her rights and just went out and did what was needed. And in the process, she held on to her own values and convictions, teaching us to do the same by her example.

So, I still don't know what it was about this woman, Muriel Duckworth. It was many things that made her who she was. But one thing I do know. Muriel was the woman we all wanted to grow up to be and the mother we all wished we had. She was a strong loving presence in our life for many years. It was a privilege to know and be involved with her.

Halifax Memorial, September 27, 2009

Anna Duckworth, Muriel's granddaughter

Around her birthday, I wrote something…
Snapshots of Granny as I knew her.
The last snapshot goes like this:

I've never dealt with death. I am twenty-four. No one close to me has died. I'm afraid — for her, for me.

Even after her hundredth birthday she's not ready. We've never talked about it — she and I. But each time death is mentioned in her presence, she squirms. She readjusts. She says nothing. Her fear is loud.

I'm preparing to lose her.
I will miss our chats.
I will miss her advice.

In her apartment we eat Cheerios and bananas for breakfast. At my place setting she's laid out a few of her birthday cards she thinks I might like. There's a Vietnamese painting on the cover of one. And the other is a black and white photo of a window in the Hive — her old house. I tell her I am worried about the world. I ask her if it'll be okay. I think she knows the answers.

What was it like to live through the Great Depression, Granny?

"If I were you, I wouldn't spend my time worrying. At your age, I'd spend my time doing what you can do that's good. Love is going to save the world. It has to be love, or the world will just go down. You work with love, don't you dear?"

I tell her I do.

It's been three weeks since the big party. She's still tired.

I wonder if she'll revive. I'm waiting for her to feel rested.

I'm afraid to lose my teacher.

* * * * *

Today I'm 25.
My teacher is gone now.
But I know it's OK.

Marion and Muriel signing books at the launch of
Muriel Duckworth: A Very Active Pacifist, House of Commons, 1996

Epilogue

Muriel's love was rooted and centred in her love for her family. From there, following her own mother's example, it spread to the communities where she grew up and later lived. Like a river, her love fed the grassroots organizations she helped to found, overflowed to her entire country and finally through her participation in world affairs reached people in every country. Her love was not abstract but remained connected to real people through her involvement in peace and political activities. She was able to identify with children, youth, women and men everywhere and to take on their cares and woes and their joys as her own. Muriel loved us individually and, by connecting so many of us to one another, has truly left us with her legacy of love.

I am grateful to Martin and Eleanor for encouraging me to speak on the phone to Muriel shortly before she died. I conveyed to her the love we all had for her.

Marion Douglas Kerans

Also by Marion Douglas Kerans

MURIEL DUCKWORTH
A Very Active Pacifist

"Muriel is an extraordinary woman whose life and work has enriched many — through her faith and her practice. A feminist, a pacifist and a compassionate Canadian, her life is an example of what love and selfless intelligence can do."
— Ursula M. Franklin C.C. FRSC

ISBN: 9781895686685
$22.95 CAD
fernwoodpublishing.ca

"Muriel Duckworth inspires me. She is living, walking proof that age need not destroy one's commitment to progressive social ideals. Muriel is a true humanitarian who freely gives herself to others regardless of their race, sex, class or ethnic origins."
— Rocky Jones, Halifax lawyer

"Muriel Duckworth's unwavering commitment to the cause of peace and human progress has inspired countless women and men. The story of her life's work will cheer and revitalize the thousands who meet her for the first time in this book."
— Alexa McDonough, former leader of Canada's New Democrats